Unveiling the Feminine Face of the Church

Helen Cecilia Swift and Margaret N. Telscher

Unveiling the Feminine Face of the Church

An Exploration for
Groups or Individuals

Nihil Obstat: Rev. Hilarion Kistner, O.F.M.
            Rev. Edward Gratsch

Imprimi Potest: Rev. Jeremy Harrington, O.F.M.
            Provincial

Imprimatur: +James H. Garland, V.G.
            Archdiocese of Cincinnati
            January 20, 1989

The *nihil obstat* and *imprimatur* are a declaration that a book or pamphlet is considered to be free from doctrinal or moral error. It is not implied that those who have granted the *nihil obstat* and *imprimatur* agree with the contents, opinions or statements expressed.

Scripture selections taken from *The New American Bible With Revised New Testament,* copyright ©1986 by the Confraternity of Christian Doctrine, Washington, DC, are used with permission. All rights reserved.

Excerpt from *The New Jerusalem Bible,* copyright ©1985 by Darton, Longman & Todd, Ltd. and Doubleday, a division of Bantam, Doubleday, Dell Publishing Group, Inc., is reprinted by permission of the publisher.

Cover and book design by Julie Lonneman

ISBN 0-86716-108-6

Acknowledgments

We wish to express our appreciation to those who read the manuscript and gave many valuable suggestions:

Joseph Bracken, S.J., Joyce Hoban, S.N.D. de N.,
Frank Oppenheim, S.J., Dr. Daniel Price, Cecile Rench,
Margaret Roalef, Beth B. Huber, Jo Anne Jones,
Dotty Purkiser, Virginia Schuster, Esther Woliver.

Contents

Introduction

Oh, no—not another book about women and the Church! Hasn't it all been said by now?

Much indeed has been said on the subject—often at the top of someone's lungs. This book is different. It is intended for ordinary Christians, both women and men, who are concerned about the Church and uneasy with radical feminism. We hope to present a balanced view of the need for women (and feminine qualities) in the Church's ministry—an approach far removed from the angry, strident attitude of some feminists.

We are not implying that women have been entirely excluded from Church ministry; their influence has been felt since the time of Jesus. But over the centuries there has been no real balance of roles for women and men—and, therefore, of masculine and feminine qualities—in the Church's ministry. Most leadership roles fall to men, for instance, and nurturing roles to women. A woman can lead—and her leadership style is likely to be different from a man's. A man can nurture—and his style is likely to be different from a woman's.

We will try to unveil the feminine face of the Church, which claims our love and fidelity, and show how it could be enriched and invigorated for *all* the People of God.

We begin by seeing what people mean when they describe certain qualities as feminine (Chapter One). The next two chapters look for such qualities in God and in Jesus. Chapters

Four and Five take a quick look at history, exploring feminine influence in the early Church and its later decline; Chapter Six focuses on the reversal of that decline wrought by the Second Vatican Council. Each of the remaining five chapters examines the need for feminine qualities in a specific area of ministry: community-building, God's Word, service, justice and sacraments.

Each chapter consists of four sections:

1) A *Case* to help you focus your thoughts and get in touch with your feelings on the subject of the chapter.

2) A *Gospel Event* that shows Jesus in relationship to the topic being considered. (You might want to use this passage for private prayer. Let the event come alive to you by placing yourself in the scene. Ask Jesus to reveal to you what this event means to him.)

3) A *Closer Look* which develops the topic and presents some ideas for your consideration.

4) An *Illustration* from the life of a person who embodies some of the attitudes or qualities discussed in the chapter. These sketches are not intended to present role models but merely to locate the chapter material in a real person's life.

Questions for Reflection follow each section. These questions relate to your own experience. Focus on those which spark a response.

A *Bibliography* offers suggestions for further reading.

Suggestions for Group Use

Individuals can use this book with profit, but their experience will be richer if they discuss it with others—with several friends, with a group to which they already belong or a group called together for the specific purpose of studying this book. Before coming together to share and discuss, we suggest that each person first read all four sections of a chapter and reflect on the questions alone.

Here are some practical suggestions:

- The size of the group is important. The ideal is eight to 12 people.
- A variety of backgrounds among the members can enrich the discussion, but remember that too great a diversity of viewpoints may create more heat than light.
- Start with an organizational meeting to settle such details as frequency of meetings, time and place, leadership (whether one person takes the responsibility or the role is rotated).
- Begin and end on time. Promptness shows respect for the purpose that brings the group together and for the time restraints of busy people.
- Limit refreshments to coffee or soft drinks. Refreshments can become a source of competition, especially if the group meets in one another's homes.

Following is a list of the leader's responsibilities.
- Begin the meeting with a prayer, a song or some icebreaker which includes all in the group.
- Since you probably will not have time to discuss all the questions in a particular chapter, ask each participant to choose five questions to discuss. Jot down each person's selections, tabulate which questions get the most votes and use these questions for discussion. (A complete listing of the questions in each chapter can be found in the Appendix.)
- Be sure no one is pressured to speak but that all are given the opportunity to share their insights.
- Shortly before the time agreed upon for ending the meeting, bring the meeting to closure with a brief summary of what has happened, an appropriate Scripture reading, a song or a prayer.

Although the leader is important to the success of the process, the attitude of the participants is perhaps even more crucial. Each member must be convinced that no one has the complete truth. Each person who speaks offers a gift to the group, and the contribution should be received with respect.

Differences of opinion should be welcome. The questions are not meant to spark arguments but to allow many viewpoints to surface. Through sharing and challenging one another to greater clarity—without trying to change anyone—all can grow to a more accepting and loving attitude toward the People of God, women and men. This attitude can bring reconciliation and set all free to contribute their talents in the Church's ministry. Then indeed God's Reign will flourish and spread throughout the world.

CHAPTER ONE

Defining Femininity

*T*here are two human sexes: female and male. Each has a cluster of dominant personality traits we consider characteristic, but both also share the full range of human qualities. This chapter will look at a few of the theories that attempt to account for sex-related personality traits. As you read, explore your own understanding of what it means to be masculine or feminine.

Case: Carl

In his middle-management position Carl is known as an ambitious, competitive, upward-moving young executive. At work he knows what he wants and goes after it with enthusiastic drive. When there are decisions to be made, Carl is consulted even by those above him on the corporate ladder, for he has a reputation for clear, logical thinking.

The other department heads in Carl's division are outwardly friendly to him. They want to be on his side, for Carl has been known to crush those who get in the way of his climb in the corporation. Several times other employees have been passed over for promotions or been downgraded to make room for Carl. As a result, while some people admire Carl for his aggressiveness and competence, others resent him.

Carl is happily married and has two preschool children.

Although he often has to work late, he tries to get home early enough to play with the children, read them a story and tuck them in for the night. He spends a great deal of time with them on weekends.

Questions for Reflection

1) How would Carl's business associates describe him? How would a neighbor, observing Carl with the children, describe him? Explain any differences.

2) How do you think Carl would feel if his business associates saw him caring for the children?

3) Do you think Carl is typical of young executives? Explain your answer.

4) At work, Carl has a reputation for clear, logical thinking. Are there other ways of thinking? Are these ways appropriate for the business world?

5) Do you usually arrive at decisions logically or by consulting your feelings? Do you always arrive at decisions in the same way? Explain your answer.

Gospel Event

And people were bringing children to [Jesus] that he might touch them, but the disciples rebuked them. When Jesus saw this he became indignant and said to them, "Let the children come to me; do not prevent them, for the kingdom of God belongs to such as these. Amen, I say to you, whoever does not accept the kingdom of God like a child will not enter it." Then he embraced them and blessed them, placing his hands on them (Mark 10: 13-16).

Questions for Reflection

1) The disciples and Jesus responded to children in very different ways. How do you explain this difference?

2) How do you think children reacted to the disciples? How do you suppose the children's mothers felt toward the disciples?

3) How do you picture children responding to Jesus? Can you sense how the mothers felt toward Jesus?

4) Do you believe that there are feminine traits and masculine traits? If so, try to list 10 of each.

5) What is the source of these traits?

A Closer Look at Femininity

We use the word *feminine* without questioning its meaning, assuming that there is some generally accepted definition. Only when we begin to examine its meaning more closely do we discover the utter chaos underlying this familiar term.

Female and *feminine* are not equivalent terms. To be female is to possess the anatomical structures and functions that make a person female rather than male. Of itself, the term *female* says nothing about a person's psychological traits or behavior. *Feminine* is the word we use to describe such things.

If we study a great many females we might discover that, in general, they are compassionate, intuitive, relational, nurturing and emotional. Not all would possess these traits in the same degree, but there would be definite evidence of their presence in most females. On the other hand, if we looked for these same characteristics in a large number of males we would find a different distribution. Males, in general, would rank lower in these traits. Most males, however, would rank higher than the majority of females on such traits as logical thinking, aggressivencss and competitiveness.

The obvious conclusion is that there are feminine traits which predominate in most females and masculine traits that predominate in the majority of males. It is important to note that *all* human traits, both feminine and masculine, appear in both men and women. In other words, no trait is so exclusively feminine that it can be said to exist in every woman and be totally absent in every man.

As early as the third century B.C., philosophers listed traits as either feminine or masculine. They did not see the two categories as complementary but rather as unequal. Once man was labeled "rational," then it followed that woman, who was obviously different, must be "irrational." As Genevieve Lloyd states in *Man of Reason*, "From the beginnings of philosophical thought, femaleness was symbolically associated with what Reason left behind."

Great thinkers—Philo, Augustine, Thomas Aquinas—described femininity as opposite and inferior to masculinity. They proposed models of maleness and femaleness and assigned mutually exclusive groups of traits to men and women.

Men, on the one hand, were thought of as reasonable, aggressive and associated with culture (the sphere of human control)—qualities assumed to be totally lacking in women, who were therefore incomplete, imperfect. Women, on the other hand, were said to be emotional, nurturing and associated with nature (the sphere of human dependence). Strange as it may seem, the infrequent appearance of these qualities in men was not seen as a lack but rather as proof of men's superiority. This view of masculine and feminine was fostered and instilled in generation after generation—even into our own time.

Our era has seen many attempts to describe and discover the roots of so-called masculine and feminine traits. In general there are two groups of theories about the source of feminine traits: the physical and the psychological.

The first group of theories—the physical—includes past observations of behavior which have led psychologists to conclude that women and men do not think alike. The psychologists' only explanation was that the female brain is somehow inferior. Recent studies of the way the two hemispheres of the brain function suggest that there *is* a difference in the way women and men think, but the "inferior" label is becoming increasingly unacceptable. More and more people recognize that *different* does not imply *inferior*.

Tests of mental capabilities show an enormous overlap in the results for women and men. A number of people can (and do) excel in activities that, on the average, favor the other sex. While there may be some basis for saying that women and men think differently due to genetic differences, there may be no characteristics inherent to the brains of either sex that necessarily limit intellectual achievements. There are so many variable factors that nothing can be predicted about the abilities or traits of any individual.

It is too early to draw hard and fast conclusions from these studies, but they may indicate that *all* humans have a range of potential behavior so broad that it is impossible to characterize behavior patterns as either male or female.

One group of psychological theories centers around the notion that trait differences between the sexes are linked to environmental factors. Those who hold these theories argue that children are not *born* with masculine or feminine traits but *develop* them as they try to live up to the expectations of parents, teachers and society. Little girls are given dolls while their brothers receive cars and war toys. Children's stories picture little girls playing house while the boys are climbing trees, playing ball and having all kinds of adventures. Girls are praised because they are cute and well-behaved, because they are "good little girls." Boys, on the other hand, are complimented on athletic skills, strength and courage.

These theories do not explain the little girl who is taught to be quiet, submissive and gentle but continues to prefer playing rough-and-tumble games with her brothers and their friends. What is the source of her aggressiveness, competitiveness, courage?

Psychologist Carl Jung proposed a psychological answer based on his clinical observations. He described the human psyche as made up of the conscious and the unconscious, with consciousness the smaller part. He then identified two layers of the unconscious. In the one closer to consciousness, the *personal* unconscious, are stored the thoughts, memories, impressions and feelings of which we are consciously unaware.

The deeper layer, which Jung called the *collective* unconscious, is formed by heredity and evolution. We know our bodies are linked with the past, so it is not surprising that Jung should theorize a similar link in our psyches. Our inherited psychic material exists in the collective unconscious as patterns which Jung called *archetypes*. Of particular interest here are the two Jung named with the masculine and feminine forms of the Latin word for "spirit": the *animus* and the *anima*.

Jung hesitated to define these archetypes, but he described the way they function. In any particular person either the animus or the anima will dominate—that is, will lie closer to consciousness, affecting everyday behavior; the other will lie deeper within the unconscious and surface less often.

The anima tends to be relational, to reach out to others, to move toward wholeness and appreciate values. It is intuitive, nurturing, compassionate and emotional. The animus functions logically, appreciates objective facts and recognizes the interconnections between them; it analyzes and discriminates. It sometimes appears competitive, aggressive and unemotional. In other words, the characteristics we identify as either feminine or masculine seem to come from the level of the unconscious where the anima and animus dwell.

One needn't be a Jungian psychologist to realize that there is something of the masculine and something of the feminine in each of us. But most of us *most often* act out of the characteristics peculiar to our sex. We do this even though we know we *can* act on the traits usually ascribed to the opposite sex.

All these sex-related personality traits have both positive and negative aspects. Reasoning and logical processes may result in opinionated views which a person holds with great conviction, often to the frustration and anger of others. Or a woman who is too nurturing can treat adult offspring like small children and even keep them unhealthily dependent on her.

The healthiest people are able to integrate the masculine and the feminine. For instance, a woman can logically (in a "masculine" way) dissect what she already perceives through "feminine" intuition; a strong ("masculine") man can display "feminine" gentleness and compassion.

In a word, for a woman the qualities and traits that are usually labeled masculine come from the unconscious (a woman's animus) to influence the behavior of women positively or negatively to a degree that varies tremendously from woman to woman. In a man, masculine qualities are more conscious and feminine qualities (a man's anima) are located in the deeper level of the unconscious.

Many people find it difficult to admit the presence of opposite-sex personality traits and do all in their power to suppress these qualities when they appear from the unconscious. Yet this is one of the factors that accounts for the unique personalities that enrich our lives. And psychologists believe that the way to wholeness—to a balanced, healthy personality—lies in recognizing and allowing all positive qualities to emerge from the unconscious. The integration of positive feminine and masculine qualities, whether from the conscious or unconscious, is one of the keys to human wholeness.

Questions for Reflection

1) As you reflect on your own personality, list 10 traits that you find in yourself. Label each trait feminine or masculine. How did you decide which traits are feminine and which are masculine?

2) Choose one feminine trait and one masculine trait that you find in yourself. Try to trace the development of these traits in your life, starting with your childhood.

3) Do you think it is important to recognize and accept both aspects of your personality—the feminine and masculine? Why?

Illustration: Golda Meir

Even to those who knew her well, Golda Meir was an enigma. Sometimes she seemed the classic Jewish mother: affectionate, caring for others, unselfish and emotional. But she also used her affection to manipulate others, to bring them around to her way of thinking. She seemed to be at ease with what others often saw as contradictory ways of behavior, affection versus manipulation, for example.

In many ways Golda's early life was not unusual. She was born in Kiev, came young to the United States and grew up in various American cities. She worked in the garment industry, taught school and studied socialism at night.

Then, when she was 23 years old, Golda went to Palestine and lived in a kibbutz. There she became well known as a tough negotiator with the British during the emergence of the State of Israel. After Israel declared its independence, Golda filled several governmental posts under David Ben-Gurion. As foreign minister she was so much in accord with Ben-Gurion's policy of retaliation against the Arabs that he remarked, "She is the only man in my Cabinet."

In 1969 when Golda was secretary general of Israel's Labor Party, she was asked to succeed the prime minister, who had died of a heart attack. In what might be characterized as a typical feminine response, she burst into tears and began talking about her family and her limitations. But this response did not deter her from accepting the position.

Those who worked closely with her often found her style confusing. For example, she would meet with members of her Cabinet over supper in her kitchen and, in that domestic scene, decide harsh measures of retaliation for Arab raids. She made tea in the early morning for her bodyguards but appeared at diplomatic functions in a severe business suit and low-heeled shoes.

Golda resigned after the 1973 October War, berating herself for failing to call for total mobilization of Israel's forces. In her autobiography she wrote, "I, who was so accustomed to making decisions, failed to make that one decision. That Friday morning I should have listened to the warnings of my own heart and ordered a call-up."

For the next five years, Golda continued to influence the affairs of her country. At her death in 1978, New York's Cardinal Terence Cooke commented: "I join with men and women of all nations of the world in expressing gratitude for the countless contributions of this renowned woman and am praying that she will now know the peace that was her life's quest."

Questions for Reflection

1) What positive feminine qualities did Golda seem to exhibit? What positive masculine qualities?

2) Would you be comfortable working with someone like Golda? Explain.

3) Have you ever known a woman in whom masculine as well as feminine qualities were highly visible?

Summing Up

Historically, masculine traits have been considered superior and feminine traits deemed inferior. It is the opinion of these authors that both society and Church need to affirm emphatically that differences do not imply inferiority for either sex but, rather, a source of richness for the world.

This book will focus on the following feminine qualities: compassion, gentleness, the ability to relate to others in a caring and feeling way, the ability to express emotions, nurturing. We believe that these traits are present in women in various degrees in a conscious way and that they are also present in the unconscious of men.

The reflection of God's goodness can be seen in both men and women. We are so accustomed to referring to God in masculine terms that we may easily overlook God's feminine qualities. In the next chapter we will explore some references to God's feminine side in the Hebrew Scriptures.

CHAPTER TWO

The Feminine Side of God

*T*he language we use to speak of God reflects male imagery. We call God "Father" and use masculine pronouns to describe "his" activity, even though we say God is neither male nor female. The Hebrew Scriptures refer to God in feminine terms, not only as the giver of life, but also as the compassionate sustainer and nurturer of life, qualities which we consider feminine. As you read, explore your own image of God.

Case: Erica

Erica, a woman in her mid-30s, enjoys proclaiming the Word as a lector in her parish church. She is aware that all pronouns referring to God are masculine, and she notices that the people of God are often addressed as "sons" or "brothers." Occasionally she changes a few words to make the language more inclusive: for instance, inserting *sisters* after *brothers*, or changing *men* to *people*. When she glances at the congregation, she sees some members smile in approval while others shake their heads and frown.

Until recently Erica wasn't troubled by the masculine references. But after taking some excellent Scripture courses, she opened her eyes to the power language has to shape thinking. Now she wants to share her insights with others.

Questions for Reflection

1) Why do you think some people are upset when Erica uses inclusive language?

2) Do you think it is important to use inclusive language at Eucharist? Why or why not?

3) Explore your image of God with this exercise: List adjectives you use to describe God. Which denote masculine qualities and which describe feminine traits? Which kind dominate your description of God?

Gospel Event

As [Jesus] drew near to the gate of the city, a man who had died was being carried out, the only son of his mother, and she was a widow. A large crowd from the city was with her. When the Lord saw her, he was moved with pity for her and said to her, "Do not weep." He stepped forward and touched the coffin; at this the bearers halted, and he said, "Young man, I tell you, arise!" The dead man sat up and began to speak, and Jesus gave him to his mother. Fear seized them all, and they glorified God, exclaiming, "A great prophet has arisen in our midst," and "God has visited his people." This report about him spread through the whole of Judea and in all the surrounding region (Luke 7:12-17).

Questions for Reflection

1) Notice phrases in the Gospel story which describe Jesus' actions: "moved with pity," "do not weep," "touched the coffin," "gave him back to his mother." What adjectives could you use to describe Jesus in this event?

2) Notice the words used by the people in the crowd: "A great prophet..."; "God has visited his people." What virtues are displayed by the people who respond this way?

3) Considering that Jesus is God, are there any hints of the divine feminine in this incident?

A Closer Look at the Feminine Side of God

In the first chapter we noted that certain qualities are usually considered feminine and others are generally thought of as masculine. We also have seen that both masculine and feminine qualities are present in every human being and that a balance of qualities is important for wholeness and health.

Since God is the source of all that is human, we would expect to find all masculine and feminine qualities in God. Yet the God revealed in the Scriptures is referred to in predominantly masculine terms.

When reading the Scriptures, we must remember that the Jewish and Christian traditions developed in cultures which were largely dominated by patriarchal customs, images and symbols. Both Old and New Testaments were written by people steeped in their cultures; naturally enough, these writers conceived of God as a Patriarch.

To balance this view, let us consider some feminine images of God which appear in the Bible.

The first book of the Bible testifies that God created humanity in the divine image:

> God created man [*ha adam*] in his image;
> in the divine image he created him;
> male and female he created them. (Genesis 1:27)

Look at the word *ha adam*, a collective noun which literally means "human," as shown by the English plural, "Let *them* have dominion..." (Genesis 1:26). You can see from the moment of creation that God intended no discrimination between the sexes. To put it another way, human nature has two expressions— female and male—and neither is superior to the other.

The Hebrew Bible contains images which present God as feminine. The prophet Isaiah describes God speaking to Israel:

> Can a mother forget her infant,
> be without tenderness for the child of her womb?
> Even should she forget,
> I will never forget you.

See, upon the palms of my hands I have written
your name;..." (Isaiah 49:15-16a)

God's motherly care does not end with childhood; God nurtures
us throughout our lives, as Isaiah makes clear:

Even to your old age I am the same,
even when your hair is gray I will bear you;
It is I who have done this, I who will continue,
and I who will carry you to safety. (Isaiah 46:4)

Jesus, weeping over the Holy City, lamented: "Jerusalem,
Jerusalem, you who kill the prophets and stone those sent to
you, how many times I yearned to gather your children together,
as a hen gathers her young under her wings, but you were
unwilling!" (Matthew 23:37).

The image of motherly care Jesus used is often found in
the Hebrew Bible. For example, Boaz blesses Ruth, a Moabite,
with the words, "May the Lord reward what you have done! May
you receive a full reward from the Lord, the God of Israel, under
whose wings you have come for refuge" (Ruth 2:12). Several
of the psalms also make use of this motherly image. Psalm 57:2,
for instance, is an appropriate prayer in time of darkness,
loneliness or danger: "In the shadow of your wings I take refuge,
till harm pass by."

In contrast to the image of God who loves and protects
in a motherly way, another image suggests strength and
courage—the eagle. When we visualize an eagle we
immediately think of power and upward flight. Imagining
ourselves borne up on an eagle's wing suggests that, from that
position, we can do what the eagle does. The eagle image carries
a sense of empowerment, dynamism and risk-taking—qualities
that have a masculine tone.

Some students of eagle behavior insist that the wings
referred to in the Bible belong to the *female* eagle. In the
picturesque words of Virginia Mollencott, the biblical translators
"made the divine mother eagle vanish into a patriarchal
confusion" (*The Divine Feminine*). In the *New American Bible*,
for instance, Deuteronomy 32:11 presents the eagle as a thing
("As an eagle incites *its* nestlings forth/by hovering over *its*

brood...") and completes the analogy by depicting God as male ("so *he* spread *his* wings to receive them/and bore them up on *his* pinions"). (The emphasis has been added.)

Some translations, however, restore the feminine. The *New Jerusalem Bible*, for example, uses the feminine pronoun in all the verses of Job 39:27-30, which concludes with the stark sentence, "Even her young drink blood; where anyone has been killed, she is there."

A powerful feminine image of God—Wisdom—is found in Proverbs, Wisdom, Job, Baruch and Sirach. In Hebrew, "wisdom" is a feminine noun. Wisdom is often personified as a mature, beautiful woman:

> For she is fairer than the sun
>   and surpasses every constellation of the stars.
>   (Wisdom 7:29)

Many biblical references picture wisdom involved in the creation of the world. For example, in Proverbs 8:27-30, Wisdom speaks:

> When he established the heavens I was there,
>   when he marked out the vault over the face of
>   the deep;
> When he made firm the skies above,
>   when he fixed fast the foundations of the earth;
> When he set for the sea its limit,
>   so that the waters should not transgress his
>   command;
> Then was I beside him as his craftsman,
>   and I was his delight day by day,
> Playing before him all the while....

Solomon, weighed down by the responsibilities of ruling and following God's command to build the temple, needed wisdom. According to the Book of Wisdom, he prayed for it:

> Now with you is Wisdom, who knows your works
>   and was present when you made the world;
> Who understands what is pleasing in your eyes
>   and what is conformable with your commands.
> Send her forth from your holy heavens
>   and from your glorious throne dispatch her

That she may be with me and work with me,
    that I may know what is your pleasure.
For she knows and understands all things,
    and will guide me discreetly in my affairs
        and safeguard me by her glory;...
                    (Wisdom 9:9-11)

The author of Wisdom knew what a magnificent gift Wisdom is:

For in her is a spirit
    intelligent, holy, unique,
Manifold, subtle, agile,
    clear, unstained, certain,
Not baneful, loving the good, keen,
    unhampered, beneficent, kindly,
Firm, secure, tranquil,
    all-powerful, all-seeing,
And pervading all spirits,
    though they be intelligent, pure and very subtle.
                 (Wisdom 7:22b-23)

Another passage from the Book of Wisdom came to be
expressed by the feminine word *Shekinah*:

For she is an aura of the might of God
    and a pure effusion of the glory of the Almighty;...
For she is the refulgence of eternal light,
    the spotless mirror of the power of God,
        the image of his goodness.
                 (Wisdom 7:25-26)

The word *Shekinah* does not appear in biblical texts, but Jewish
rabbis used it as early as the first and second centuries B.C. to
refer to the residence of God's presence with the people. In
early Hebrew literature the flame enveloping the unburned
bush, the cloud over Mt. Sinai, the cloud resting upon the
tabernacle during the day and the fire at night were all
understood to be *Shekinah*—a relational caring, a feminine
manifestation of God.

    In contrast to the hovering presence of God Isaiah 61:8
and Proverbs 8:16 picture Wisdom as very active, working in
the public arena, striving to bring about justice in human affairs.
Wisdom brings feminine influence to balance the masculine

qualities usually associated with public life. The balance needed for wholeness for individuals and for the world is symbolically expressed in Wisdom 7:27-28:

> And she, who is one, can do all things,
>   and renews everything while herself perduring;
> And passing into holy souls from age to age,
>   she produces friends of God and prophets.
> For there is nought God loves, be it not one
>   who dwells with Wisdom.

Questions for Reflection

1) What is your clearest image of God? Is that a masculine or feminine image?

2) Which biblical images of God appeal to you most? Why?

3) What effect do you think stressing masculine images of God has had on Christianity?

4) How can reflecting on the feminine images of God enrich your relationship with God?

Illustration: Ann Sullivan Macy

Ann knew what it means to struggle against great odds. As a child of 10, she lost both father and mother. Sent to the almshouse at Massachusetts State Infirmary at Tewksbury, Ann lived for four years in abject poverty with substandard care. An inspector investigating the conditions at the almshouse recognized Ann's inner strength and deep desire for an education. Through the inspector's efforts Ann, who was losing her sight, was sent to the Perkins Institute for the Blind. There she learned to read Braille. Only later, after several eye operations, was Ann able to read normally, and then only for limited periods.

After graduation from Perkins Institute as valedictorian, Ann was hired by Captain Arthur H. Keller as tutor and companion to his daughter, Helen, left blind and deaf by a childhood disease. Unable to see or hear or speak, Helen had lived nine years in a world apart, a "phantom existence," she

21

later characterized it. Everyone but her parents had given Helen up as a hopeless case. Helen herself referred to March 3, 1887 (the date when Ann arrived in the Keller home), as her soul's birthday: for Ann Sullivan Macy—"Teacher"—introduced Helen to language and put the girl in touch with the world.

Working so hard with Helen, Ann gradually lost more of her own sight and her health began to fail. Reading became more and more difficult for Ann as she continued her own education in order to further Helen's. Ann spent endless hours translating what she had read into finger language for Helen. As Helen became more skillful and began creating literature herself, Ann wrote down her pupil's words until Helen learned to use a typewriter.

Dr. Alexander Bell, who befriended and encouraged Ann and Helen, recognized that Helen's astonishing progress was due to the gifts of *two* unusual people. Ann was bright, creative and enthusiastic, and Helen was persistent and unquenchable in her desire to learn. Almost literally Ann was willing to give her life's blood to satisfy Helen's thirst.

Ann was not a "religious" person, as she declared again and again to Helen. Ann attended no official Church and downplayed the importance of such connections in Helen's life. Because of her regard for Helen's freedom and independent thinking, Ann did not interfere with Helen's religious convictions.

Toward the end of her life, Ann seems to have gained a glimmer of hope in immortality. In a biography of Ann, Helen quotes her beloved Teacher shortly before Ann's death:

> I have wasted time grieving over my eyes. I am
> very, very sorry, but what is done is done. I have
> tasted the bitterest drop in my cup, but if you are
> right about God and immortality, we can be sure
> that He will not allow to perish great thoughts, grave
> thoughts, thoughts lasting to the end....Lying here
> in the hospital I feel that I am at the feet of God.

For some time after Ann's death on October 20, 1936, Helen felt disoriented, that she could not go on creatively without Teacher. Then she remembered what Ann had said: If Helen did not go on, Teacher would have failed no matter what great things had been accomplished previously. This remembrance of Ann Sullivan Macy's faith in her sparked Helen's energy and Helen continued her great accomplishments.

Questions for Reflection

1) How does the relationship between Ann and Helen mirror the feminine qualities of God?

2) In what ways have specific persons in your life brought you to new psychological and spiritual growth?

3) In what relationships have you called forth life in others?

4) How would you characterize the early relationship between Ann and Helen? Did this relationship change? Have you had any similar experiences?

Summing Up

In an attempt to enter into the mystery of God in a balanced way, we have explored in this chapter a few feminine images of God from the Hebrew Scriptures. Several prophets as well as psalms refer to God not only as the giver of life but also as the sustainer, nurturer and protector of life—qualities which emphasize the feminine image of God. God's compassion (a distinctly feminine characteristic), strength and risk-taking (masculine qualities) are symbolized by the wings of various birds.

Wisdom is the feminine-gender image used to describe God's activity in creation, in the journeys of the chosen people, in the public arena of life. At times it shows the connection between the Hebrew and Christian Scriptures.

With this view of God as background, let us look briefly at the influence of the feminine in the ministry of Jesus.

CHAPTER THREE

The Feminine Side of Jesus

*I*n the last chapter we considered God's feminine qualities. Since Jesus is the Word of God come to live among us, we might expect to find both masculine and feminine qualities in him. This expectation does not negate his masculinity, for Jesus, being truly human, shared masculine qualities with all men. But he also possessed qualities we consider feminine. As you read, reflect on the feminine qualities evident in Jesus' public life.

Case: John

John, a college graduate in his late 20s, has decided he wants to help people, to do something worthwhile with his life. At one time he thought he might have a priestly vocation, but after prayer and consultation he decided that God was not calling him that way.

For the past three months John has been working at a shelter for homeless men. People off the streets come to the shelter in the early evening for a hot meal, a bed for the night and breakfast the next morning. John believes that homeless men have feelings, too, and will respond to kindness. John talks to the men as they enter the shelter and goes to the recreation room to watch TV and chat with them in the evening. John's approach is quiet and gentle, and the men realize his concern for them. They respond to his care.

Now John may lose his job. The shelter director has explained to him: "John, you can't act this way around here. You have to be tough with these hard street bums. When you talk to them as they come in, you hold up the line. We've got to be more organized—get them in here, feed them and get them to bed as quickly as possible. You can't make them feel like they're welcome here; they'll keep coming back. My God, John, you almost *mother* them!"

Questions for Reflection

1) Is John's way of treating the homeless appropriate? Why or why not?

2) How do you feel about the director's attitude toward the homeless who come to the shelter?

3) Are there unspoken implications in the director's statement? If so, what do these implications tell you about the director?

4) Imagine yourself in John's place. What would you do?

5) Think of five persons you encountered in the past week and reflect on your interaction with each one. Was the person a woman or a man? What qualities did this person call forth from you? Did you feel you were your true self with this person, or did you respond the way you thought the person expected? What was the outcome of this encounter for each of you? How do you explain any differences among the five encounters?

Gospel Event

The tax collectors and sinners were all drawing near to listen to him, but the Pharisees and scribes began to complain, saying, "This man welcomes sinners and eats with them." So to them he addressed this parable. "What man among you having a hundred sheep and losing one of them would not leave the ninety-nine in the desert and go after the lost one until he finds it? And when he does find it, he sets it on his shoulders with great joy and, upon his arrival home, he calls together his friends and neighbors and says to them, 'Rejoice with me because I have found my lost sheep.' I tell you, in just the same way there will be more joy in heaven over one sinner who repents than over ninety-nine righteous people who have no need of repentance" (Luke 15:1-7).

Questions for Reflection

1) Is it reasonable that a man would leave 99 sheep untended and unprotected to go in search of one? Why or why not?

2) What kind of man is Jesus portraying in this parable?

3) What does Jesus reveal about himself and his Father in this parable?

A Closer Look at the Feminine Side of Jesus

Psychologists say the way to wholeness is to integrate both the conscious and unconscious elements in our personality. The path to wholeness requires careful discernment—the ability to recognize and sift out what leads us to act in certain ways. Sometimes we discover why we acted in a particular way only *after* the fact. How much more valuable is the ability to recognize our tendencies and *choose* the motivation for our actions. Then discernment leads to responsible decisions and, gradually, to wholeness.

But that assumes an ability to recognize unconscious qualities, which is in itself difficult for many people. Further, it sometimes takes courage to name such qualities and claim them as part of oneself.

People who reject some qualities in themselves usually reject them in others. For example, a man's inability to be in touch with his own feminine qualities can cause him to be judgmental of men who respond to a situation in feminine ways. This lack of understanding may result in conflicts, as John discovered. A woman who does not accept her unconscious masculine qualities may be critical of assertive women, calling them aggressive and harsh.

The process of discernment also reveals that not everything coming from the unconscious has positive value, that some impulses or desires should not be acted upon. We need to recognize and accept the qualities from which such impulses flow even as we strive toward appropriate Christian action. Wholeness is achieved by integrating those elements that have positive value into one's personality. This discernment is the work of a lifetime—and even then few people arrive at perfect balance, perfect harmony between the conscious and unconscious.

There is a wholeness to Jesus' personality. Perfect inner freedom allowed him to respond to people in an appropriate way. Therefore, we find Jesus at times displaying some very masculine characteristics—for example, wielding a whip in the Temple (John 2:14-16)—and at other times responding to a situation in a feminine way—for instance, embracing a child before placing it in the disciples' midst (Mark 9:36-37).

To clarify how he would respond to people, how he would carry out his mission of proclaiming the Reign of God, Jesus went into the desert to prepare for public life. It is not easy to understand what Jesus meant by the "Reign of God." William Barry, S.J., cofounder of the Center for Religious Development in Cambridge, Massachusetts, describes it as the "intention of God that all human beings live as brothers and sisters in a community of faith, hope and love, united with Jesus Christ as sons and daughters of God in harmony with the whole created universe." We might picture Jesus as he went into the desert, facing an urgent problem: "How do I tell people what God wants for them on earth and in heaven?"

The temptations in the desert represent possible approaches, approaches that wield power in a negative masculine way. The temptation to turn stones into bread was just one instance when Jesus might have abused masculine power over material things: to manipulate people in order to bring about God's Reign. But Jesus resisted that temptation and allowed a feminine quality to surface: a deep appreciation of spiritual values. He acknowledged that there are greater values in life than material things.

The second temptation offered the power of political

domination. The tempter implied that, if Jesus ruled the world, he could establish the Kingdom easily. If Jesus had that kind of power, he could make people do what he wanted; people would have to accept his will because he held control over their lives. Again, Jesus recognized that the Father's will lay in a different approach to people.

The temptor presented to Jesus a third way of using power, a means based on people's false expectations of the Messiah. Many Jews believed the Messiah would appear in such an unusual way that no one would know his origin. Uneducated people are especially vulnerable to the magical; they follow anyone who can mystify them, fascinate them by doing extraordinary things. What could be more spectacular than descending from the roof of the Temple surrounded by God's protective power? What an effective way of forcing belief! Again Jesus rejected the temptation to manipulative power.

Throughout his time in the desert, Jesus recognized that his Father's will was for him to proclaim the Kingdom in the context of loving relationships. Jesus was to have compassion for the "little people," those who resembled children in their simple faith. In other words Jesus was to allow the feminine qualities within him to be active in his proclamation of the Kingdom.

Jesus came out of the desert to proclaim God's Kingdom. Secure in his own freedom, he approached people in ways that respected the freedom of his listeners. He understood from his time in the desert that he was to appeal to the people in a nonthreatening way, to announce to them that God was active in the world and in their lives.

The people of Jesus' time belonged to a storytelling culture, so Jesus used parables to help them understand God's action. The parables usually had one point which could be understood by those open to Jesus' message. Many parables presented a paradox, an idea to provoke the listener to think about new possibilities, new ways of looking at life.

A number of Jesus' parables teach us what God is like. In this sense it has been said that Jesus himself is a parable, for we can see in the care he shows for the oppressed, for marginal people, for women, for those suffering in mind and body, how

God cares for all of us. In expressing those qualities of caring and compassion, Jesus allowed his feminine side to emerge.

Some parables Jesus told seem to be addressed especially to women. He cared about women and their concerns. He used simple, homey incidents to illustrate the profound truths of the Kingdom. He spoke of a woman's satisfaction at seeing yeast affect dough. He used this daily experience of women to stress how God's remarkable activity penetrates and enlivens everything with a touch. A woman's gratification when she sees dough rise gives us a sense of God's rejoicing at the spread of the Kingdom in the world.

As a parallel to the story of the lost sheep, Jesus tells of a woman looking for a lost coin (Luke 15:8-10). He could feel the distress of a poor woman whose dropped coin disappears some place in the room. She would sweep in the corners and under the simple furniture until she retrieved it. Jesus did not hesitate to compare his heavenly Father's joy with the joy of this woman. Jesus not only empathized with a person doubly oppressed—as woman and as poor—but he wanted his listeners to know that God also cares.

By his actions as well as by his words, Jesus let his listeners know that the Kingdom was already present in the world. The Kingdom points to human wholeness, and Jesus modeled what that wholeness looks like. It was important to Jesus that people realize the love and merciful forgiveness of his Father, but it was not enough to *tell* them. Jesus showed them by his *actions* how much God cares for the human family.

At the beginning of his public life, Jesus was invited to a wedding. His mother was also a guest at the wedding and, as such, had no responsibility for the refreshments. Women notice little details, however, and Mary saw that the supply of wine was low. She was concerned for the young couple, not wanting their celebration to be marred by embarrassment. When Mary expressed her concern to her son, Jesus first responded, "Woman, how does your concern affect me?" (John 2:4).

Then he somehow recognized that his mother's concern was his concern also. Mary, in tune with her son, was not surprised; she had already told the servants to follow her son's instructions. Jesus, of course, did become involved. And when the chief steward tasted the water made wine, he was confused. He stated the reasonable custom of the time: "Everyone serves good wine first, and then when people have drunk freely, an inferior one; but you have kept the good wine until now" (John 2:10). The masculine approach is to do the logical thing, but in this case Jesus responded from feminine sensitivity to the feelings of others.

John the evangelist calls Jesus' act a "sign." In John's Gospel *sign* has a special meaning: a miracle which encourages belief and, at the same time, reveals Christ's true character. John makes clear the importance of this miracle: "Jesus did this as the beginning of his signs in Cana in Galilee and so revealed his glory, and his disciples began to believe in him" (John 2:11).

All four evangelists record Jesus' miracles; some miracles— for example, the healing of a blind man—can be found in all four Gospels. It is evident that Jesus' miracles are important to his mission—but not because they are unusual or spectacular. Rather, what is of value for us is the *meaning* of a miracle: its effect on the person who experienced it and what it reveals to us of Jesus and his message.

Jesus did not heal all the blind, deaf, sick and afflicted in the villages and towns where he preached. Those who were cured usually had an attitude which Jesus called *faith*. They were willing to trust God's action in their lives. They demonstrated belief that their lives were not completely at their disposal but that their existence had a deeper meaning. They were open to the new possibilities that God opened up through Jesus.

If we look closely at the way Jesus responded to this openness, we find that he often cured people in a feminine way. When the lepers came to him for healing he did not stand at a safe distance but reached out and touched them, a feminine gesture.

When Jairus came to Jesus begging for his daughter's cure, Jesus went home with him. On the way, a woman reached out and touched his cloak, a very bold action for two reasons. According to Jewish custom, a woman was forbidden to touch a rabbi. Because she was bleeding, she also was ritually unclean and would bring anyone she touched into the same state, an even graver violation of Jewish tradition.

Jesus was very sensitive; he knew that energy or healing power had gone out of him. There was no indication that Jesus was angry or even uncomfortable at being touched by this woman. He could have let her disappear into the crowd to rejoice over her cure in private. Why then did he insist that she reveal her identity? When Jesus assured her that her faith had healed her, both she and the bystanders knew that the cure was not magical, but Jesus' gentle response to the faith he found in this woman. Public revelation also indicates that the woman was fully healed, socially as well as physically. The crowd knew that she was no longer ritually impure, that she was now free to participate in the synagogue community. Arriving at the house of Jairus, Jesus did not allow the neighbors' ridicule to arouse his anger. He was concerned about the little girl. Mark makes a point of recording that the girl was 12 years old, the age when a girl became a woman under Jewish law. Jesus did not hesitate to touch her. In a motherly gesture, he took her by the hand, saying, "Little girl, I say to you, arise!" (Mark 5:41). In the midst of the rejoicing that must have followed, Jesus thoughtfully reminded her family to give her something to eat.

Many Gospel examples reveal Jesus' respect, appreciation, understanding and love for women. In *Unpopular Opinions*, writer Dorothy L. Sayers reflects on what Jesus must have meant to the women he met:

> [Women] had never known a man like this Man— there never has been such another. A prophet and teacher who never nagged at them, never flattered or coaxed or patronized; who never made arch jokes about them...who rebuked without querulousness and praised without condescension...who never mapped out their sphere for them, never urged them to be feminine or jeered at them for being female; who had no axe to grind and no uneasy male dignity to defend; who took them as he found them and was completely unself-conscious. There is no act, no sermon, no parable in the whole Gospel that borrows its pungency from female perversity; nobody could possibly guess from the words and deeds of Jesus that there was anything "funny" about woman's nature.

Questions for Reflection

1) How do you feel about reflecting on Jesus in terms of modern psychology?

2) Find several passages in the Gospels that show Jesus' masculine traits in contrast to the feminine qualities presented in this chapter. What other miracles do you feel reveal his masculine qualities? How do they differ from the ones cited in this chapter?

3) How do you understand the "Kingdom" or "Reign" of God? Does your description of the Kingdom contain both feminine and masculine aspects?

4) Read slowly Dorothy L. Sayers' comment about Jesus. How do you feel about Jesus as you read this?

Illustration: Teilhard de Chardin

Pierre Teilhard de Chardin was a noted paleontologist (one who studies ancient geological ages through fossil remains), respected and esteemed by other scientists. He was also a Jesuit priest and, most of all, a man of deep faith.

Born in 1881 and reaching maturity in a time when the opposition between faith and science was still very much alive, Teilhard was able to integrate his scientific thought with his religious beliefs—but not without a struggle. As a young religious, Teilhard felt torn between his fascination with the study of the material cosmos and his loyalty and devotion to the supernatural. As he struggled to reconcile within himself his two great loves—of God and of matter, he became convinced that God and Christ could be found in all things in the world, even in the marvels revealed by modern science. Therefore one could serve God and Christ by laboring in this new world of the technocratic age.

To some people this sounded like the traditional doctrine of the "good intention": encountering God in daily life by seeking God's will even in ordinary things. This doctrine seemed to imply that *what* is done is unimportant and that the *motive*, seeking God's will, is what counts. But Teilhard believed that *what* is done is also important to God's plan for the earth. We need to look not just at the motive of our work but also at our choice of particular work. We need to ask, "How is my work contributing to the progress of human beings and the earth on which we live?" Progress, to Teilhard, meant that all creation is moving toward that fullness of being that God intended. He was convinced that holiness and wholeness are synonymous.

Teilhard stressed God's creative action through this evolution of the earth. Human endeavors and achievements are important in bringing ourselves and our world to fulfillment: This is the way God is at work in the universe. In his *Hymn of the Universe* Teilhard expressed this belief, addressing God:

> I am in very truth in contact—and the closest possible contact—with the two aspects of your creative activity; I encounter and I kiss your two wonderful hands: the hand that lays hold on us at so deep a level that it becomes merged, in us, with the sources of life, and the hand whose grasp is so immense that under its slightest pressure all the springs of the universe respond harmoniously together.

This is just one way Teilhard expressed traditional Catholic beliefs in new ways. Often misunderstood by his superiors, he was forbidden to publish his ideas and was exiled from Paris to China in 1926. His superiors recognized his competence in his scientific field and so never restricted his strictly technical and scientific publications.

For his part Teilhard was a loyal Jesuit priest, obedient to his superiors and to the Church. Early in life he expressed his conviction: "Blessed are they who suffer at not seeing the Church as fair as they would wish and who are only the more submissive and prayerful for it." In a letter written toward the end of his life, Teilhard insisted that he had lived out this early conviction. He said, "In truth (and in virtue of the very structure of the whole of my thought), I feel myself today more irrevocably bound to the hierarchical Church than I have ever been at any point in my entire life."

Questions for Reflection

1) What similarities do you find in Teilhard's approach to his mission and Jesus' desert preparation for his?

2) Do you believe that Teilhard followed the example of Jesus in carrying out his mission? If so, in what ways?

3) Do you find any evidence that Teilhard was in touch with his unconscious feminine traits?

4) Are there any similarities in the consequences of Jesus' and Teilhard's loyalty to their respective missions?

5) Do you believe that Teilhard's attitude toward the Church is relevant for Catholics today? Why or why not?

Summing Up

Many incidents in Jesus' life show his perfect freedom to express either masculine or feminine qualities. We see in Jesus what it means to be a complete human being, to hold the masculine and the feminine in perfect balance with none of the traits repressed or expressed in a negative way.

We chose Teilhard de Chardin to illustrate the theme of this chapter because in his life the masculine and feminine are beautifully blended. His sharp scientific mind delved into the mysteries of nature and his masculine way of thinking enabled him to make important contributions to scientific thought. At the same time his feminine sensitivity gave him deep insight into and appreciation of the most insignificant bits of creation. He well understood that holiness means wholeness in the image of Christ and union with Christ.

In this chapter we explored the feminine side of Jesus, the Church's founder. In the next chapter we will look at efforts in the early Church to maintain the truly revolutionary attitude toward all that is feminine which Jesus exhibited in his life.

CHAPTER FOUR

Feminine Influence in the Early Church

*I*n the days immediately following Pentecost many women brought their feminine gifts to the early Church. Their contribution faded from memory over the centuries, but it can still be traced through ancient documents. As you read this chapter, reflect on the role women have played in shaping the Church you know.

Case: Christa and John

The young couple listened attentively as their pastor announced that the permanent deacon program would begin soon in the diocese. Both Christa and John were active in St. Andrew Parish and had a great desire to deepen their own spiritual life. They had developed a strong relationship with one another and with their young children. They felt that God had gifted them and they wanted to reach out to those in need. It was important to them that they minister together. The deacon program seemed to be the answer they were seeking.

They made an appointment with Father Downing to get more details about the diaconate. As they listened to their pastor describe the program, they realized that only John was eligible to become a permanent deacon. Christa would not be welcome as a full participant in the program nor could she be ordained. The pastor tried to console her by telling her that she could participate in some other ways. The young couple went away from the rectory crestfallen. Together they decided that John would not apply for a place in the deacon program either.

Questions for Reflection

1) Do you share in the disappointment experienced by Christa and John? Why or why not?

2) Why do you think that Christa was not welcome to participate fully in the permanent deacon program?

3) Do you believe that the People of God would benefit more if Christa and John could work together than if John ministers alone as a permanent deacon? Why or why not?

4) From your observation, are more men or more women actively involved in ministry in your parish? Can you think of reasons why this is true?

5) Are there any ministries that you think are being neglected in your parish? If so, what can you do to remedy the situation?

Gospel Event

But Mary stayed outside the tomb weeping. And as she wept, she bent over into the tomb and saw two angels in white sitting there, one at the head and one at the feet where the body of Jesus had been. And they said to her, "Woman, why are you weeping?" She said to them, "They have taken my Lord, and I don't know where they laid him." When she had said this, she turned around and saw Jesus there, but did not know it was Jesus. Jesus said to her, "Woman, why are you weeping? Whom are you looking for?" She thought it was the gardener and said to him, "Sir, if you carried him away, tell me where you laid him, and I will take him." Jesus said to her, "Mary!" She turned and said to him in Hebrew, "Rabbouni," which means Teacher. Jesus said to her, "Stop holding on to me, for I have not yet ascended to the Father. But go to my brothers and tell them, "I am going to my Father and your Father, to my God and your God." Mary of Magdala went and announced to the disciples, "I have seen the Lord," and what he told her (John 20:11-18).

Questions for Reflection

1) What do you suppose Mary meant to do when she reached the tomb? Was this reasonable?

2) Do you believe that a compassionate response is usually called forth by a reasoning process? Why or why not?

3) How do you feel when your friends call you by name? Is your response similar to Mary's?

4) How do you suppose Mary felt as Jesus said, "Stop holding on to me"?

5) How do you think Mary felt when she heard Jesus say, "Go...and tell them..."? When have you been sent to bring the Good News to others?

6) Bernard of Clairvaux once called Mary Magdalene an "apostle to the apostles." Do you think this is a good title for Mary? Why or why not?

A Closer Look at the Early Church

The story of the Church immediately following Jesus' Resurrection is told in the Acts of the Apostles, some of Paul's epistles and portions of John's Gospel. During the first centuries Clement, Ignatius of Antioch and Polycarp wrote letters which have also come down to us. These sources present the infant Church as small communities of people coming together to share their memories of Jesus, to support one another in their attempts to live the "new way" and to follow Jesus' Last Supper command to break bread as he did. Their vision of Jesus and his message motivated the first Christians to work together in community to bring about the Kingdom Jesus had preached.

Any organization—including the Church—that hopes to run smoothly needs to have people filling different roles. These people must work together in unity and cooperation; competition among them often results in hostility and alienation. A common vision which enables members to move corporately toward a common goal creates unity and cooperative action. As we shall see in more detail in later chapters, the ability of people to form communities is vital to the health of the Church. Women played a major role in forming the first Christian communities.

Women more easily form groups or communities because relationships are a higher priority for them than for men. Psychologists tell us that this ability to relate to others begins early in life. The mother-daughter bond is very strong because little girls identify with their mothers. Girls thus develop a relational quality. The mother-daughter bond is the basis for feminine desire and ability to form deep relationships.

The mother-son bond, on the other hand, requires the son to distance himself from his mother in order to achieve a male self-identity. This process results in masculine independence and self-assertion and a lessened tendency toward community formation. With this difference in mind, let us consider how women responded to the events immediately following the death of Jesus.

On Easter morning a small group of women went together to the tomb. Even though they knew Jesus had died, they still experienced so deeply their relationship with him that they put aside their fears and ventured into the predawn darkness— only to find the tomb empty. The Gospel accounts vary in some details, but they agree that the women were sent to tell the apostles of Jesus' Resurrection. Although they are not mentioned specifically in later Resurrection appearances, these brave women hardly would have been excluded from subsequent experiences of Jesus' presence.

After Jesus ascended into heaven, according to the Acts of the Apostles, the disciples returned to the upper room in Jerusalem. Some women were among their number and, when the house shook on Pentecost, "they were all filled with the holy Spirit and began to speak in different tongues, as the Spirit enabled them to proclaim" (Acts 2:4).

Perhaps familiarity with this passage has caused us to miss

the significance of *all*. The Holy Spirit apparently made no distinction among the disciples gathered in prayer. Men and women were equally enabled to proclaim the Good News, each in the way the Spirit led.

The Acts of the Apostles and some of Paul's epistles mention by name some women who were active in the early Church. In Romans 16:1-16, the conclusion of his letter to the Church in Rome, Paul sends special greetings to women who have assisted him in his ministry: Phoebe, "minister of the church at Cenchreae...a benefactor to many and to me as well"; Prisca, a coworker in Christ Jesus who had risked her life to save Paul; Mary, "who has worked hard for you" and the woman who is Rufus's mother "and mine." These and other references make it appear that these women were working *with* Paul, not just *for* him. Yet, though Phoebe, Prisca and Mary ministered side by side with Paul, they were never mentioned with the apostles like some of their male counterparts.

The women mentioned above probably belonged to a group referred to as *devoti*, "devoted ones," the name given to those who tried to live out the Gospel ideal without compromise. Groups of *devoti* made up of both men and women were part of the Jerusalem community after Pentecost. These groups extended gradually into the wider Church and became the heart of many of the house churches.

Acts 9:36-42 tells the story of Tabitha, a Joppa convert who "was completely occupied with good deeds and almsgiving." The Christian community of Joppa was so grieved at Tabitha's death they sent for Peter, who raised her from the dead in a scene strikingly similar to Jesus' raising of Jairus's daughter (see Chapter Three).

The same passage in Acts mentions "the widows" as a special group of Christians. These women greeted Peter on his arrival in Joppa, displaying the clothing Tabitha had made "while she was with them." After restoring life to Tabitha, Peter presents her to "the holy ones and the widows."

The Church in the East still regards the Order of Widows as the "mother form" of women's groups formally organized for service in the Church. This group was made up of women whose husbands had died or who, for some reason, were separated from their families—women who had no means of support other than the local Church. In order to receive such support a woman had to be an exemplary Christian (see 1 Timothy 5:7-15). The widows were known for holiness of life, for prayer and for service. These women were chosen by the Church and enrolled as widows by a special consecration. A fifth-century document called the *Testamentum Domini* contains a prayer for their consecration—their ordination, as it was then called.

Such women were under the leadership of the bishop. Unlike later religious orders, these women were not set apart by different garb or enclosed behind cloister walls. They were very much involved in the world around them and noteworthy because they lived the Christian ideal so intensely. They tended to live together according to a common rule which included daily prayer and frequent Eucharist.

The widows were recognized as part of the hierarchical structure, ranking after the three male orders: elders, bishops and deacons. They never held a special function in worship, however. They were essentially charismatic and were ordained for "presidency" over women in the general life of the Church, chosen for office because of their spiritual and womanly gifts. Although they shared their gifts with other Christian women, the Church as a whole was deprived of their feminine influence. These women, mainly from the middle and upper classes, had much to offer, but they were impeded by cultural and religious restrictions on their ministry simply because they were women.

In the third century the Order of Virgins—women who chose to remain virgins—was given official recognition. As more and more virgins were absorbed into ecclesial orders of women, asceticism gained emphasis over service. Prayer and rigorous fasting began to predominate among the widows. No longer was service to the community considered important or even necessary.

This rigorist spirit led many to unorthodox Gnostic and Montanist heresies. Because of such tendencies, the women were subjected increasingly to closer control. Teaching or preaching roles were denied them, and silence in church and marketplace became their lot. Utterly dependent on the support and goodwill of the bishop, the widows, who had once been outstanding for their teaching and ministerial service, now were restricted to personal prayer and rigorous living. Forced to turn their attention on themselves, the widows were sometimes thought demanding and grasping and so opened themselves to sharp rebuke by Church authorities. By the year 360 the Order of Widows was decreed no longer an ecclesiastical state in the Eastern Church.

In the East another important group of women in the early Church were *deaconesses*. The Order of Deaconesses was a clerical order described extensively in the *Didascalia*, a third-century document, and again in the fifth-century *Apostolic Constitutions*. Both documents distinguish between the Order of Widows and the Order of Deaconesses. The Council of Nicea in 325A.D. listed deaconnesses as clerics, ranked between deacons and subdeacons. The prayer for their ordination, proclaimed by the bishop with his hands laid on them, is very similar to the one used in ordaining deacons.

Some scholars have argued that deaconnesses were not *really* ordained. Yet these early documents testify that deaconesses performed the same services for women that deacons did among men. They were charged with instructing the newly baptized women, visiting the sick and even with baptizing women. They were regarded by all as associates of the bishop.

In the Western Church women were less active. Although widows became quite numerous in the early Western Church as well, feminine influence there took a slightly different form of development. By the middle of the third century there were 1,500 widows in Rome, according to a letter from Cornelius to Bishop Fabian of Antioch. Particularly in Rome and Carthage, however, the Order of Widows early evolved into the diaconate and these women instructed women preparing for Baptism.

Many widows and virgins in the Western Church lived and worshiped at home, joining together only for Eucharist. Some widows lived in community; in certain ways, they foreshadowed religious life as we know it today. Both groups, although not separated entirely from the world, made vows and wore distinctive garb as a public sign of their consecration.

In the fourth century Augustine wrote about widows and virgins and how they lived, striving for holiness of life mainly through ascetical practices, prayer and response to Christ in terms of human love. Augustine emphasized strongly their need to be faithful to Church and to community life. He mentions some holy women by name: Monica, his own mother, and Juliana, a widow praised in his treatise *The Excellence of Widowhood.* Jerome also stressed the virtue of fidelity in his exhortations to the widows of Rome. Not all the widows were poor and needy women. Jerome's widowed friends—Marcella, Paula and Fabiola—were neither poverty-stricken nor alone. They came from high social positions and wished to consecrate their widowhood to the service of God's people through prayer and works of charity.

Although the widows of the Western Church engaged in many of the same activities as the deaconesses of the Eastern Church, they were never given the same high ecclesiastical status. By the fifth and sixth centuries various canons (Church laws) include strong words limiting the activities of the devoted women, admonishing them and even prohibiting them duties they formerly performed. Subsequent documents occasionally mention exceptions but, by the end of the 11th century, deaconesses no longer existed. Although vestiges of women's ecclesial status survived longer in the Eastern than in the Western Church, by the beginning of the 13th century they had disappeared there, too.

The nuns who replaced the deaconesses were, in fact, a new creation, not an adaptation of an old one. Nuns in monasteries pursued holiness by separation from the world, not by rendering service. In the Church of the Middle Ages, women who sought holiness without compromise were confined to the cloister, thus restricting their ministry to the spiritual area. As the centuries moved on, women more and more sought to combine the activity and service of the deaconess with the cloistered nun's striving for holiness.

Questions for Reflection

1) The early Church developed a model of ministry in which men and women worked together in service to the Christian community. What evidence of such cooperation do you observe in your own parish? What evidence of competition between the sexes do you see in your parish?

2) Envision ways Christianity can further cooperation rather than competition. Who in your parish exemplifies such a vision?

3) What feminine qualities help to bring about cooperation rather than competition?

4) How could the women of your parish help create a more Christian community?

5) If deaconesses were once so prominent in Church ministry, why do you think women are now excluded from the permanent diaconate?

Illustration: Simone Weil

If Simone Weil had lived during the first century, she would have felt at home in the early Church. As a 20th-century philosopher, however, she never overcame the intellectual barriers that prevented her from being baptized.

Born of Jewish parents in Paris in 1909, Simone was an extremely intelligent girl whose favorite pastime was discussing ideas. She had few friends her own age, for few could keep up with her intense search for truth.

This search for truth led her down diverse paths. Her wanderings were fueled by a burning desire to know the truth about God. She felt she shared with the early Christians "the problem of knowing how to view God's creation of the world." She believed that some passages in the Gospels and in Paul's letters place God and the world in opposition. She asked herself how this could be true if God had created the world.

Just as the early Christians struggled together for a deeper understanding of the life, death and resurrection of Jesus, so Simone constantly sought people who would reflect with her on her religious dilemmas. She was drawn to the Catholic Church and, during the last years of her life, often went to Mass. But she felt she had to solve her intellectual questions about Christianity before she could be baptized. She made a list of 35 of her "heresies," as she called them, and sent them to a priest friend, hoping that in his reply she would find the truth she so desperately sought.

Simone was convinced that her particular vocation demanded of her the greatest possible intellectual honesty. Toward the end of her life she wrote: "It is for the service of Christ as the Truth that I deprive myself of sharing in his flesh in the way he has instituted. He deprives me of it, to be more exact, for never up till now have I had even for a second the impression of there being any choice."

Questions for Reflection

1) In what ways was Simone like the early Christians? In what ways was she different?

2) Why do you think Simone felt she had no choice in putting off Baptism?

3) What masculine qualities do you see in Simone? What feminine qualities?

4) How have you carried out your search for truth?

Summing Up

In this chapter we have seen how many women once enriched the Church with their gifts. Feminine relational qualities were at work in forming the early Christian community. Following the example of Jesus women gave priority to serving the poor and needy; this kind of ministry appealed to their compassion and generosity. Especially in the Church of the East, groups of women were given ecclesiastic status; they exerted a powerful influence on the development of the early Church. These women soon felt the restrictions and limitations placed on them by men. Patriarchy, which we will look at next, had already taken root in the earliest days of the Church.

CHAPTER FIVE

The Decline of Feminine Influence

As the Church entered the mainstream of society, the surrounding culture exerted more and more influence on it and patriarchy gradually emerged. The simple sharing of the early followers of Jesus was replaced with structures characterized more by dominance rather than service. Women, subservient to men in the larger society, were reduced to obedience and silence in the institutional Church. As you read, reflect on the nature of authority in the Church.

Case: Carlos

A group of Brazilian peasants gathered regularly in a base community to read and share the Word of God. In the neighborhood lived a man named Carlos, who was shunned and isolated because he had committed heinous crimes during his life. Murder, rape and robbery were all part of this man's story. Now he was quite ill, and an old hammock swinging between two trees in the village was the only place he could lay his head. One of his daughters brought him a bowl of rice each day, barely enough to keep him alive. No one loved him and he was left alone to suffer and to die.

One day the leader of the base community opened the

Scripture to the parable about the barren fig tree (Luke 13:6-9). As they came to the words of Jesus, '[I]t may bear fruit in the future," the community thought of the man in the hammock. They remembered another lesson from Scripture: that "nothing will be impossible for God" (Luke 1:37). The community recognized a call from God to help the one they had come to hate.

As was their custom when a job was to be done, the leader asked for volunteers to perform the necessary tasks. One man contacted the nearest hospital to request an ambulance and reserve a bed for the dying man. Another man volunteered to ride with Carlos in the ambulance to the hospital. Several people were charged with bathing Carlos and providing clean clothing for his emaciated form. In an unbelievably short time all was ready and the people then joined in prayer for Carlos's well-being.

Shortly after his arrival in the hospital, Carlos died. The people of his village prayed that he had heard the words of Jesus on the cross, "Amen, I say to you, today you will be with me in Paradise" (Luke 23:43).

Questions for Reflection

1) In what ways have you heard God's call as you prayed over Scripture passages?

2) These peasants were neither Scripture scholars nor theologians. What does this tell you about the power of the Word of God?

3) In your parish what pastoral activities could be assumed by lay women and men? In what areas would feminine qualities enrich this pastoral care?

Gospel Event

There was a scholar of the law who stood up to test him and said, "Teacher, what must I do to inherit eternal life?" Jesus said to him, "What is written in the law? How do you read it?" He said in reply, "You shall love the Lord, your God, with all your heart, with all your being, with all your strength, and with all your mind, and your neighbor as yourself." He replied to him, "You have answered correctly; do this and you will live."

But because he wished to justify himself, he said to Jesus, "And who is my neighbor?" Jesus replied: "A man fell victim to robbers as he went down from Jerusalem to Jericho. They stripped and beat him and went off leaving him half-dead. A priest happened to be going down that road, but when he saw him, he passed by on the opposite side. Likewise a Levite came to the place, and when he saw him, he passed by on the opposite side. But a Samaritan traveler who came upon him was moved with compassion at the sight. He approached the victim, poured oil and wine over his wounds and bandaged them. Then he lifted him up on his own animal, took him to an inn and cared for him. The next day he took out two silver coins and gave them to the innkeeper with the instruction, 'Take care of him. If you spend more than what I have given you, I shall repay you on my way back.' Which of these three, in your opinion, was neighbor to the robbers' victim?" He answered, "The one who treated him with mercy." Jesus said to him, "Go and do likewise" (Luke 10:25-37).

Questions for Reflection

1) What feminine qualities did Jesus show in his conversation with the lawyer?

2) Why do you think the priest and the Levite passed by the man?

3) The Jews looked upon the Samaritans with contempt. In his story why do you think Jesus chose a Samaritan to help the injured traveler?

4) Who might 20th-century Americans look upon as Samaritans? Why?

A Closer Look at the Decline
of Feminine Influence

Jesus left an example for the early Church: both his own freedom
to act in either a masculine or feminine way and also his attitude
toward women. From the very beginning, however, there was
tension between the Christian vision of a discipleship of equals
and the patriarchal culture.

The patriarchal household was the basic unit of society
in Jesus' time. The father was head of the family; wife, children,
servants and slaves were all legally dependent on him. The
right of inheritance belonged to the eldest male. When the early
Christians began thinking of themselves as a new family and
worshiping as house Churches, they were unconsciously
planting the roots of a patriarchal structure.

Scholars do not agree on precisely what it means to say
that Jesus "founded" the Church. They do agree that Jesus
preached that the Reign of God is present, although yet to come
in its fullness. This Reign and the salvation it brings are open
to all who believe and live the Good News.

At various times during his public life Jesus sent his disciples
out to preach what he had taught them. After his Resurrection
Jesus gave Peter the repeated command, "Feed my lambs....Feed
my sheep" (see John 21:15-17). He commissioned the disciples
to proclaim the Good News: "Go, therefore, and make disciples
of all nations, baptizing them...,teaching them to observe all
that I have commanded you" (Matthew 28:19-20a). Jesus' *intent*
for his disciples seems clear but not the method his followers
were to use to organize themselves for the task.

We have some indication of the way Jesus looked on
authority. When Zebedee's sons asked Jesus for positions of
power, Jesus used the opportunity to explain to his disciples
how they were to use authority: "You know that those who are
recognized as rulers over the Gentiles lord it over them, and
their great ones make their authority over them felt. But it shall
not be so among you. Rather, whoever wishes to be great among
you will be your servant; whoever wishes to be first among
you will be the slave of all" (Mark 10:42-44). It seems evident
then, that to Jesus power and authority were closely associated

with service and not to be exercised by domination or with an arrogant attitude of superiority.

Such an understanding prevailed as long as Christianity was a marginal sect. Because some Christians believed that the Spirit of the living Jesus breathed where it willed, they began to speak out with authority. When such speaking became widespread, distortions of Jesus' message began to occur. The apostles and later the bishops began to exercise restraint over this movement. Authority became institutionalized in the bishops. All those not duly ordained in the developing hierarchical system were held to silence.

Conflict also arose when a group of Christians (Gnostics) began preaching that matter was evil and that the Reign of God would only come about in a future life. Other Christians saw these teachings as contrary to their belief that God had created all things good and that Jesus had proclaimed the Kingdom already present *and* yet to come. Eventually the Gnostics were declared heretics by those recognized as having authority in the Church.

Thus the bishops gradually assumed a role resembling the father of the family. The patriarchal society of the time became the model for the growing Church. So development within the Church itself paved the way for the next step—the growth of a hierarchical system that had no place for women.

The conversion of Constantine and the incorporation of Christianity into the Roman Empire in the fourth century had perhaps more to do with the present hierarchical structure than any other single factor in history. When Christianity became the state religion, it was almost inevitable that Roman influence would be felt in the Church. The simplicity of the early Christians was replaced by the manners and customs of the Roman court. The exercise of authority gradually began to conform to Roman structures; the celebration of the Eucharist and the proclamation of the Gospel became complex and burdened with elaborate rituals. For special ceremonies the pope, bishops and priests dressed in rich, ornate vestments resembling the trappings of earthly rulers. They grew more and more distant from the people they were meant to serve, and the patriarchal system became more and more entrenched in the Church.

Another factor which strengthened patriarchy can be discovered in theological writings. Augustine in the fourth century and Aquinas much later in the 13th century profoundly influenced the Church's (and the clergy's) attitude toward women. They refer to women as dangerous: seducers of men, whores whose very presence preys upon the masculine psyche. Church Fathers and canonized saints through the centuries equated womankind with the harlot, the temptress; at times some even questioned whether women are fully redeemed. Man is seen as the "real" human being and woman as the "misbegotten male," as God's small mistake.

Obviously, this kind of thinking reinforced male domination in the Church and excluded women from positions of authority or decision-making. The role of deaconnesses and abbesses grew more and more restricted. In the sixth century the Council of Epaon abolished the Order of Deaconnesses.

Over the centuries attitudes toward women did a slow reversal. By the 19th century women had become identified with the spiritual and altruistic impulses in human behavior. They were therefore put on a pedestal and segregated—protected—from the world of male materialism and power. Femininity and Christlikeness were both relegated to a private realm of otherworldliness. The art of the period depicts Jesus in sentimental poses and often with feminine features. Love, once described by Jesus as a fire which is all-consuming, became smothered in sentimental phrases and images. Womanly qualities, while now admittedly appropriate for redemption, were considered highly unsuited for the exercise of any power or authority in the Church or anywhere else.

And so women found themselves imprisoned in two opposing views: Either they were everything weak in human nature, or they were the "higher" expression of humanity. Either view excluded them from full participation in Church ministry.

The feminine spirit was never crushed, however, but continued to exert some influence in the Church. Believers could not forget that it was Mary's assent to God which allowed the Word to become flesh; nor could they forget Jesus' attitude toward women during his public life. Some women managed to break through the barriers set up against them.

52

The great women mystics broke through the barriers by their writings, which give evidence of extraordinary favors bestowed on the Church through God's revelations to them. These women mystics experienced God as neither male nor female. Julian of Norwich went so far as to proclaim Jesus himself as both father and mother. A variety of medieval mystics—Hildegard, Mechtilde of Magdeburg, Mechtilde of Hackeborn, Gertrude and Julian of Norwich—contributed in unique ways to creation spirituality. (*Creation spirituality* emphasizes the goodness and beauty of God's creation and calls forth attitudes of praise and thanksgiving.)

A few women exerted influence in a more political way. Catherine of Siena rebuked popes and other members of the hierarchy, insisting that the pope return from his exile in France and take his place in Rome, the center of Christendom. Joan of Arc was called from obscurity to lead the French army to victory against the English. In spite of all she had done for France and for the Church, she was tried as a heretic and burned at the stake. Teresa of Avila reformed her Carmelite Order. Her writings were so valuable to the Church that she was eventually declared a Doctor of the Church.

In recent centuries hundreds of women founded religious congregations to serve the poor, the sick and the uneducated. In our own century Theresa of Lisieux became Patroness of the Missions, although she never set foot outside of the convent she had chosen as her home.

These women are exceptions who, like bright lights, pierced through the darkness of the patriarchal system and kept the feminine alive in the Church.

In the middle of the 20th century the Second Vatican Council opened the way for radical renewal and new thinking about patriarchy. The Vatican II documents on the Church, *Lumen Gentium* and *Gaudium et Spes*, called *all* the people of God to holiness. In many respects the documents recognized the dignity of women and their equality with men. Many absurdities in the writings of respected theologians of the past are now contradicted by the documents of Vatican II.

Yet the hierarchical structures of the Church remain male. Authority and the power of decision remain firmly within the grasp of male bishops and priests. The recently revised Code of Canon Law, the law of the Church, continues to exclude women from many roles in the Church.

Recently, however, efforts have been made by U.S. bishops to establish channels through which the voices of women may be heard. The bishops released the first draft of a pastoral response to women's concerns, *Partners in the Mystery of Redemption*, on April 12, 1988. Its introduction outlines the writing process: "On the basis of reports received from national hearings and from diocesan listening sessions, we have chosen to discuss the concerns raised by Catholic women....We begin with a presentation of what we have heard....We then explore what our heritage provides in response to main themes....Finally, we try to respond appropriately to what we have learned" (*Partners in the Mystery of Redemption*, #19).

In October of the same year Pope John Paul II issued an encyclical which reaffirmed the Church's longstanding teaching that Christ himself excluded women from ordination—a position many theologians and Scripture scholars still question.

Meanwhile, the constantly decreasing number of duly ordained priests results in large segments of people throughout the world being deprived of life-giving sacraments: Eucharist, Reconciliation, the Sacrament of the Sick. The question has been raised: Are we facing a time when we can no longer be spiritually nourished on a regular basis by the Eucharist?

We are moving in the direction of becoming a Church which cannot celebrate Eucharist. Of the 19,500 U.S. parishes, 10 percent now have no resident priest. Looking at seminary enrollments makes the picture even more bleak; too few men are preparing for the priesthood to replace the priests who will die or retire.

Questions for Reflection

1) Where does the power of decision rest in your parish?

2) Are both men and women well represented on your parish council? How are the members selected?

3) Is it necessary to have structure in an institution as large as the Roman Catholic Church? How and by whom should decisions be made within such a structure?

4) In your lifetime have you observed a lessening of patriarchy in the Church at any level—parish, diocese, universal Church? Present the evidence.

5) In what ways has the decreasing number of priests affected your life?

Illustration: Elizabeth Bayley Seton

Elizabeth Bayley Seton experienced many roles in her life: She was wife, mother of five, widow and vowed religious. In that last career she founded the American Sisters of Charity at the beginning of the 19th century. Early in the order's history she experienced an injustice at the hands of Church authority and felt compelled to speak out.

Elizabeth and a number of her young sisters found great comfort and instruction from their spiritual director, Father Pierre Babade, S.S., a holy priest who had guided them since their entrance into religious life. He also had been responsible for the religious instruction of the pupils entrusted to their care.

Then another Sulpician, Father William Dubourg, was appointed superior of the newly formed community. Arbitrarily he forbade the sisters to have anything more to do with Father Babade. Elizabeth appealed to Archbishop Carroll in a letter which sounds like it was written by a major superior of the 1980s. (At the time canon law did not safeguard sisters' rights to freedom in matters of conscience.) Her clear-sighted realization that Dubourg's action was unjust prompted the letter even though she vowed loyalty to her lawfully appointed superior.

As a consequence of Elizabeth's stand, a number of the Sulpicians became hostile to her. The incident also caused great anguish and divisions among the sisters and other people associated with them. Father Dubourg resigned as superior of the community and resisted all Elizabeth's attempts at reconciliation. Never satisfactorily resolved, the incident stands as a symbol both of male domination in the Church and of the courage with which some women faced injustice.

Questions for Reflection

1) Has your loyalty to a parish priest or bishop ever been challenged by an apparent injustice? If so, what have you done about it?

2) Do you know people who have spoken in opposition to an unjust act? How have you responded to such people?

3) Do you believe it is possible for a good Christian to have a radically different point of view than a pastor or bishop? How can such contrary views be expressed in a respectful and open manner?

4) How do you view dissent in the institutional Church?

Summing Up

Women were reduced to obedience and silence—their state in civic life—as the Church became a large and powerful institution. Women no longer were regarded as copartners in proclaiming the Reign of God but only as assistants in the ministry controlled by bishops and clerics, who were the decision-makers. During the centuries following Christ a number of women exerted significant influence in the history of the Church and were recognized for their sanctity, but they were exceptions.

In the following chapter we will see more clearly how the documents of Vatican II opened the door for women to new possibilities in ministry.

CHAPTER SIX

Vatican II and Rewaking the Feminine

*T*he Second Vatican Council wrought many changes in Catholic thought and life. It began to reclaim the feminine side of the Church, and it opened new doors for women's participation. As you read, reflect on the role of women in today's Church.

Case: Bill and Sue

One Sunday morning Bill's and Sue's pastor gave a homily referring to the Church as Holy Mother Church. He expanded on this image at great length. Bill liked the homily, even though it was a bit long, but he noticed that Sue squirmed and sighed audibly several times.

When they were in their car waiting to get out of the crowded parking lot, Bill said, "That was a great homily, but he could have made it a little shorter."

Sue snorted. "Great! You've got to be kidding, Bill!"

Exasperated, Bill did not try to hide his feelings. "Aren't you ever satisfied? You're always talking about feminine issues— what could be more feminine than motherhood? I like to think of the Church as my mother. What's wrong with that, for heaven's sake?"

"That's because the Church treats *you* as an adult, not a child!" Sue snapped. "Let's go home!"

Questions for Reflection

1) Would you have reacted to the homily more like Bill or like Sue? Why?

2) What does the image "Holy Mother Church" imply to you?

3) Do you think it is important what image we use for the Church? Explain.

4) List the images of the Church you have heard or encountered in your reading. Next to each image list as many qualities associated with that image as you can. Which image of the Church appeals to you most? Why?

5) Does any one image imply all the qualities you look for in the Church? If not, what qualities are missing from your favorite image?

Gospel Event

Jesus returned to Galilee in the power of the Spirit, and news of him spread throughout the whole region. He taught in their synagogues and was praised by all.

He came to Nazareth, where he had grown up, and went according to his custom into the synagogue on the sabbath day. He stood up to read and was handed a scroll of the prophet Isaiah. He unrolled the scroll and found the passage where it was written:

> "The spirit of the Lord is upon me;
>   because he has anointed me
>   to bring glad tidings to the poor.
> He has sent me to proclaim liberty to captives
>   and recovery of sight to the blind,
>   to let the oppressed go free,
> and to proclaim a year acceptable to the Lord."

Rolling up the scroll, he handed it back to the attendant and sat down, and the eyes of all in the synagogue looked intently at him. He said to them, "Today this scripture passage is fulfilled in your hearing" (Luke 4:14-21).

Questions for Reflection

1) As Jesus describes his mission in Isaiah's words, what strikes you about the passage?

2) How do you see the mission of Jesus being continued in the world today?

3) Quoting Isaiah, Jesus summarizes his mission in terms of the poor, captives, the blind and prisoners. If Jesus were describing his mission today, what other groups of people might he mention?

4) Why do you think all the people in the synagogue were so fascinated with Jesus?

A Closer Look at the Effect of Vatican II

John XXIII had been Pope only 90 days when he startled the Church and the world by announcing his plan to convoke an ecumenical council. In the opening address on October 11, 1962, Pope John spoke optimistically of the Church's future and of his own hopes for the Council. He emphasized the world's need for mercy and thus set a pastoral tone for the Council.

Since that historic day, volumes have flowed from the 16 documents given to the Church and to the world by the Council. Every area of Christian life has been touched in some way by the power of the Spirit at work in the Council. In this chapter we will consider just one area: the Council's effect on women's role in the Church.

Before the Council opened a commission drafted the *Dogmatic Constitution on the Church*. This draft reflected the only understanding of the Church—a hierarchical structure— accepted both by theologians and by ordinary Catholics at that time. Laypeople at the time considered themselves *members* of the Church, but the very word *Church* conjured up images of the pope, bishops and priests who somehow *were* the Church.

The Council Fathers rejected that first draft entirely and produced a second draft which stressed a radically different understanding of Church. This new draft reflected the pastoral attitude called for by Pope John in his opening address.

The first chapter, "The Mystery of the Church," moves the focus from the hierarchical image. After considering the mission of Jesus, his death, resurrection and sending of the Spirit to dwell in the Church, the document briefly presents various images of the Church. Almost all these images have biblical roots; at some time one or more of them had special significance in the Church's self-understanding. Jesus himself offered some of them to express his relationship to his followers: the sheepfold, the vine with its branches.

The Epistles refer to a building with Jesus as the cornerstone, the house of God, the household of God, the holy temple, the Holy City, the New Jerusalem. In Ephesians and again in Revelation the Church is called the spouse whom Christ loves and looks to for love in return. An image popular in modern times comes from St. Paul: the Mystical Body of Christ. Pius XII's encyclical *Mystici Corporis* spoke to many hearts' experience of close union with Christ, highlighting the union of the Head with each of the Body's members.

Perhaps a hundred years from now Christians will look back and discover that one of the most insightful achievements of Vatican II was to stress another image of the Church. It has taken us 2,000 years to realize the power of the profound insight expressed in the First Letter of Peter: "Once you were'no people'/ but now you are God's people..."(2:10).

By discussing what it means to be "the People of God" before taking up a description of the Church's hierarchical structure, the Council Fathers initiated a new way of thinking about Church: reflecting on the Church's mission in the context of that understanding. As the Council progressed, the role of the laity took on greater significance. The documents on the Church, ecumenism, missionary life, Christian education and the liturgy all touch on lay coresponsibility for the Church's mission. Finally, after five years of intensive preparation, editing and rewriting, the Council Fathers accepted the *Decree on the Apostolate of the Laity.*

It is interesting to note that the lay apostolate dates from the time of Jesus, yet it was not until November 1965 that the Church's thinking on the subject was promulgated in a conciliar decree. Before then the rather widespread attitude was that the pope, bishops and priests were responsible for the mission of the Church. The laity were the *object* of the mission, to be ministered to by the hierarchy. The Council proclaimed the news that hierarchy and laity alike are the People of God, together charged with carrying out Christ's mission.

Throughout, the document refers to the participation of the laity as the "apostolate of the laity" or the "lay apostolate." During the years immediately following Vatican II, women, especially members of religious congregations, heard the message. They responded energetically and enthusiastically to the call to participate more fully in the mission of Christ. Curiously, however, the word *apostolate* disappeared from their vocabulary in less than five years. By 1970 a new word had surfaced: Women and men began referring to their "ministry"; that word soon became entrenched in the vocabulary of laypeople involved in the mission of Christ. The importance of this development to the way many women think about themselves and Church can hardly be exaggerated.

A shift in language is always an important sociological event. Sometimes the shift comes about deliberately through the efforts of certain groups (for example, the cry for inclusive language in the liturgy). At other times the shift occurs almost unconsciously (like the rise of the word *ministry*) and is hardly noticed until later. However the change occurs, it opens up new ways of thinking and poses new questions.

Ministry is now used to specify an ever-growing variety of justice and peace activities, works of mercy and liturgical roles. Most religious professionals now refer to their jobs as their ministry. But, strange as it may seem in the light of frequent usage, the word is seldom defined. People seem to assume that everyone understands what it means and also that all use the term in the same way. Few people who speak of "my-ministry" feel the need to define what they mean; fewer could explain why they say *ministry* rather than *apostolate.*

Well-known theologians have studied what the early Church meant by *ministry.* Theologian Bernard Cooke distinguishes five categories of ministry which will form the basis of the rest of this book: (1) ministry as formation of community, (2) the ministry of God's word, (3) ministry as service to those in need, (4) the ministry of God's judgment and (5) the ministry of the sacraments. In the early Church these ministries were closely related to the gifts of members of the community. During the rise of partriarchy, when education was at a low ebb and learning was centered in monasteries, the hierarchy gradually claimed the majority of ministries and allocated them to the clergy.

In our complicated society the growing shortage of priests makes this limitation of ministry to the ordained impossible. Bishops everywhere recognize the need for more lay participation, yet many people (and some bishops) refuse to accept the term *lay ministry.* They insist that only priests and bishops can minister; the laity can only serve.

When a word becomes so much a part of the culture that it is generally used without definition, it has already become laden with some unspoken assumptions. A careful look at Cooke's categories reveals one such assumption: All the baptized can minister. Only one of Cooke's categories— ministry of the sacraments (and not all of them at that)— requires ordination.

Questions for Reflection

1) Do you believe that you are co-responsible for the mission of Christ? If so, what is your responsibility? How do you carry it out?

2) For each of Cooke's five categories, list as many specific ministries as you can. Compare your list with the lists of other group members.

3) Do you feel that you have a ministry in the Church? Why or why not?

4) Do you believe that a baptized Christian can minister to others without being officially appointed to the ministry? Why or why not?

An Illustration: Catherine de Hueck Doherty

As a young Russian baroness Catherine faced poverty and near-starvation in her flight from Russia after the communist revolution. Years later, when she had become a noted lecturer and was making $20,000 a year on the Chautauqua circuit (a fortune for those days), she was haunted by the call to give up everything and share life with the poor.

She traced the beginnings of this call to her childhood. As a small child at Our Lady of Zion Convent school in Ramleh-Alexandria, Egypt, she often had prayed at a shrine of St. Francis in the convent yard. Her teacher told many fascinating stories about St. Francis, and Catherine promised herself that someday she would be just like Francis and live with the poor. The dream became a reality when Catherine voluntarily chose to live and pray in the slums of Toronto. A few people soon joined her and the first Friendship House began serving soup to the poor.

Catherine faced many challenges of heroic proportions in her life—as a nurse in World War I, as a visitor to Warsaw on assignment from *Sign* during World War II. But perhaps her greatest suffering came when she moved from Toronto to Harlem and began working for interracial justice in 1940. As a child she had been taught to look upon every person as someone of dignity, worthy of respect. In Harlem she agonized over the contradictions she saw in those dedicated to preaching the Gospel. She could not believe the prejudice so many Christians held against the Negro.

Sometimes Catherine was asked to lecture in the South on interracial justice. A passionate speaker, she often was pelted with rotten eggs and ripe tomatoes. After one lecture the crowd tore her clothes and left her black and blue from the blows she received. Her response to those who warned her not to go South was, "If you are going to preach the gospel with your life, you have to preach it everywhere. You can't say, 'I'll preach it in New York but not in Georgia.'"

63

In Harlem she carried on what she called the "chitchat apostolate" as she walked the four blocks from her apartment to Friendship House each morning. She described this apostolate in *Fragments of My Life*:

> When I walked by the store owners and their salesclerks were busy sweeping the sidewalks, washing windows, cleaning their stores, and getting ready for the day's work. I simply made it a point to stop at each place, or step inside if they were not working outside. At least I would stick my head through the door and bid them a cheery good morning and ask how business was doing.
>
> As time went on, this led to longer conversations....Over a period of time I got to know all about the families of the clerks and the owners. We had the most cordial relations and, if I may say so, even deeply friendly ones....This is why it took me almost three-quarters of an hour to make a trip of four blocks. Out of this chitchat apostolate, the identification with the people took place—always the hardest part of any apostolic work.

Questions for Reflection

1) What kinds of ministry do you find in Catherine's story?

2) What difference do you think Catherine saw between her poverty as a refugee and her poverty in Harlem?

3) If Catherine were beginning her work in Harlem today, what do you think she would call her "chitchat apostolate?"

4) Do you believe Catherine's "chitchat apostolate" was really ministry? Why or why not?

Summing Up

In this chapter we have looked briefly at some of the effects of imaging the Church as the People of God. Focusing on this image has caused a shift in language and a change in the way women understand their role in the Church.

In the next chapter we will look at the first of Bernard

Cooke's categories of ministry: the ministry of community formation. We will explore how both feminine and masculine qualities are necessary for the formation of ideal Christian communities.

CHAPTER SEVEN

The Feminine and the Ministry of Building Community

What makes community possible—especially in an individualistic society? This chapter will explore how feminine and masculine traits contribute to the formation of community. As you read, recall the good community-builders you have known.

Case: Carol

Carol is a lawyer with a big dream—a worldwide dream. She is contacting lawyers in every part of the world—lawyers with an interest in human rights, the environment, peace and reconciliation. She is proposing that they do advocacy research and brief-writing for Third-World people who cannot afford a lawyer. They will not defend people in foreign courts, but they will help prepare the defense.

So far Carol has a long list of lawyers who are willing to donate their time and talents but not many requests for their services. Now she is planning a three- or four-year pilgrimage through the Southern Hemisphere to locate spots where volunteer lawyers are needed most. She will visit Africa, India,

Singapore and South and Central America. She calls her trip a "working pilgrimage"—going from place to place to discover how First-World lawyers can serve.

After spending some time in a Third-World country, each volunteer lawyer will return home with a broadened perspective. Carol expects these lawyers to see defects in their legal system, failures which work injustice on the poor both at home and in foreign countries.

Questions for Reflection

1) Would you call Carol's working pilgrimage a "ministry"? Why or why not?

2) What qualities must Carol have to make her dream come true? Are these qualities feminine or masculine?

3) Do you consider the group of lawyers which Carol has recruited a community? Why or why not?

4) What is your definition of community? Using your own criteria, list all the communities to which you belong and rank them in the order of their importance to you.

5) What criteria did you use in ranking the communities to which you belong?

6) Were you responsible for forming any of these communities? If so, what was your contribution?

7) Are you a leader in any of these communities? What responsibilities do you have as a leader?

8) Next to each of the communities you have listed, indicate the qualities that are important in a member. Are these qualities masculine, feminine or a combination of both?

Gospel Event

The apostles gathered together with Jesus and reported all they had done and taught. He said to them, "Come away by yourselves to a deserted place and rest a while." People were coming and going in great numbers, and they had no opportunity even to eat. So they went off in the boat by themselves to a deserted place. People saw them leaving and many came to know about it. They hastened there on foot from all the towns and arrived at the place before them.

When he disembarked and saw the vast crowd, his heart was moved with pity for them, for they were like sheep without a shepherd; and he began to teach them many things (Mark 6:30-34).

Questions for Reflection

1) What qualities of community do you find in this incident?

2) Do you find any qualities of a genuine community missing in this event?

3) It is obvious that Jesus is the leader of the apostles' community. How does he show his leadership? How do the apostles respond?

4) What adjectives would you use to describe Jesus' leadership? Do these adjectives describe masculine or feminine traits?

Looking Closer at Community Formation

Vatican II had profound and immediate effects, especially on women. Its stress on human dignity and its emphasis on the Church as People of God caused women to think differently of themselves and of their place in the world. Married women began to face such issues as birth control, working outside the home, redefining husband/wife roles, having greater autonomy—issues with endless implications for themselves and for family, friends and coworkers.

One immediate effect of the Council was the beginning of renewal in congregations of women religious. The place of women religious in the Church is unclear. Popular thinking at times groups them with the clergy and at other times with the laity. Women religious do belong to the laity, yet canon law treats them very differently from other laypeople.

For the most part these women took the documents seriously and began looking at their congregations in light of them. No area of life was allowed to escape from their critical scrutiny.

The first obvious change was in dress—a change which caused considerable controversy both in and out of religious congregations. In retrospect it's easy to see the cause of the upset: To many people, traditional religious garb symbolized preconciliar conformity; it expressed uniform thinking and acting rather than the uniqueness of each personality in the community.

Less evident to Catholics at large was the change in the concept of community going on within congregations. In many ways, the internal structure of religious congregations was patterned on the hierarchical structure of the Church. Although there were some attempts to recognize the feminine—the superior was called *Mother*General rather than *Father*General— for the most part, the method of operation was paternalistic.

Once these structures were changed, women religious began studying in depth the more basic questions of community spirit: the charism of the foundress or founder, the formation of local communities and other questions relating to their own congregational sense of community. Basic to this renewal process was the effort to become more deeply immersed in Gospel values. We saw Jesus invite his small community to come to a quiet place with him, testifying to a community's need for bonds of loving support. Nevertheless, a community cannot become closed in on itself, concerned only with its own life. When Jesus saw the crowd seeking him so earnestly, he did not hesitate to break off intimate conversation with his close friends and carry on his mission.

Congregations which have continued to renew shifted emphasis from internal community structures (how the members relate to one another) to community in mission (how the community carries on the mission of Jesus).

The same thing is happening in the wider Church. Many women express a growing desire for community. They are coming together in a great variety of small groups for Bible study, shared prayer and support of one another in many difficulties—divorce, grief, child-rearing. Many women attest that they find within these small groups a sense of community, at least temporarily. Many also will admit, however, that something seems to be missing. They are looking for something more, although it is usually not clear just what that "more" might be. This lack of clarity is understandable; *community* is as ambiguous a word as *ministry.*

American philosopher Josiah Royce pointed out three conditions required for what he called a "genuine Christian community":

1) Becoming a community of memory and hope. The individual must move beyond the narrow confines of self to find other individuals with common interests, beliefs or ideals. He or she must further accept some events of the past that are held in common by the group. This requires one to make one's own some part of a community's life that was not part of one's own physical life, becoming able to claim such events and say, "That event *is* part of my life." The community can then begin to see new possibilities for itself and for its members.

In this way the early Christians were drawn together by accepting the passion, death and resurrection of Jesus as somehow part of their life. In the early Church, as they met and interpreted for each other the life and death of Jesus, they came to know that new life was available to them in the saving power of Jesus. They shared a vision of what it meant to be a Christian and became a community of hope in a future resurrection as well as a community of memory.

2) Becoming a community of interpretation. When individuals with some identification with past events and a common vision of some future events come together, communication deepens their bonds. Such communication is, of course, more than talking about superficial topics—the weather, sports. It involves interpreting shared memories. For example, a support group of single parents share the personal struggle to raise children alone; they share their feelings of anger, frustration, helplessness, how they cope with fatigue and financial difficulties. In a word they share the meaning of their lives.

But even this sharing is not enough. They must move beyond their personal experiences to historical awareness of the social implication (of, for instance, an increase in the number of children growing up in single-parent homes).

The vision of the early Church would have been sterile if
its members had been satisfied to turn in on themselves,
complacent in their belief that they had been saved. The
common vision should have motivating power, moving the
community to cooperative action.

3) Becoming a community of love transformed by the Spirit.
Before a community is a *Christian* community, there must be
a bond of love—a love given by the Spirit to unite the individual
members to Christ and to one another. This same Spirit
challenges the members to reach out in reconciliation to erring
members. The community then becomes a living entity, greater
than the sum of its individual members. As such, it deserves
the love and loyalty of the members.

Even this brief discussion of Royce's conditions for genuine
Christian community reveals how difficult it is to form such a
community. Many people do not realize that they are seeking
this kind of community. They only know that they are searching
and are often disappointed when their unconscious
expectations are not met.

How can today's Church fill the need people feel for
community? The first of Royce's requirements—becoming a
community of memory and hope—seems easily met. There *is*
a body of beliefs and ritual that Christians generally claim as a
part of their individual lives. The celebration of the sacraments,
especially the Eucharist, and the turn of the liturgical seasons
should give members a feeling of belonging. Yet the
individualistic spirit pervading our society may inhibit even this
first step to community formation. What should be the basis
for community—accepting the story of Jesus as part of one's
own story—is sometimes seen as an individual's means to
salvation.

Efforts to form community can break down even further
when faced with the second requirement—communication. The
very size of many parishes makes it difficult to interpret the
experience and hopes of parishioners. When people do not
even know the names of those they worship with each Sunday,
they are a long way from the kind of open communication
that builds community. Even in smaller parishes the spirit of

individualism mentioned above is an obstacle to the communication that might take place.

One by-product of this individualism is the insecurity that dominates so many people. Think of the many TV commercials offering security—better locks and alarm systems, insurance for every possible disaster or accident. Sometimes the American people seem almost obsessed with fear and the need to build barriers against anyone who might harm them. In this kind of atmosphere it is very difficult to promote the open communication so vital to forming community. And so many persons find something missing in their lives.

As we saw in Chapter Seven, giving priority to relationships is a basic feminine quality—and a prerequisite for community formation. Any person, male or female, who lacks this desire for relationships may live an isolated, individualistic and selfish life. (Isolation, of course, doesn't necessarily mean physical isolation. Some people are very involved in business, social and even family life but never let the deeper concerns and feelings of others become part of life.)

Once a community is formed, another feminine quality—intuitiveness—becomes important. This quality allows people to sense the tensions and stresses that are almost certain to arise in any group. Most women and some men are sensitive to tensions within a group, to feelings and body language. For the continuation and growth of the community these sensitive members also must develop the skill of smoothing out differences.

Women tend to be more verbal. They more readily can express their own feelings and articulate the feelings of others. Often it is the women who keep communication moving in a group. Because of their greater need for relationships, women often invest more in a community and therefore are motivated to foster the communication that makes the community viable.

At the same time it seems that loyalty to the community is something that many women find difficult. They may readily realize the support they get from the community and welcome the growth nurtured there. What they find difficult to believe is their importance to the community. In fact many women have such low self-esteem that they struggle with the notion that they are valuable in themselves, that they have something to offer to the others. They find it almost impossible to believe that this community would lack a certain dimension of richness if they were not a member.

The masculine quality of loyalty is the antidote to this low self-esteem. Men and women with a strong sense of loyalty are necessary for the continuation of the community. Loyalty shows their own love for this new entity. But these community members have another important role to play: They can foster self-esteem in those who need it by showing these members that they *are* valued, they *do* contribute to the good of the community and they *are* missed when absent from the group.

Questions for Reflection

1) Reflect on each of the communities to which you belong, applying Royce's criteria for genuine community. What conclusions do you draw from your reflection?

2) Do you think Royce's criteria are too idealistic? Why or why not?

3) Make a list of masculine and feminine qualities necessary for a viable community. What does this list tell you about the members?

4) Do you believe it is difficult to form genuine community? Why or why not? What would you find most difficult and how might you go about resolving this difficulty?

5) Why is community formation an important ministry in the Church? Do you think you have gifts for this kind of ministry?

Illustration: Elizabeth Cady Stanton

When Elizabeth Cady Stanton moved with her husband and their children to Seneca Falls, New York, in 1847, she found her life changing and her frustrations growing. "Our residence was at the outskirts of town," she wrote of this time. "I had poor servants and increasing number of children....Novelty of housekeeping had passed away...; domestic life was now irksome. My duties were too numerous and varied." Suffering mental hunger and a lack of stimulating companionship, Elizabeth often mentioned feeling lonely, depressed, angry and exhausted.

One day during the summer of 1848 as she had tea with Lucretia Mott and three other women, Elizabeth shared her frustrations and her pent-up anger at the unjust situation of women. The women sitting around the table made up their minds, then and there, to call a convention to state their grievances and find sympathizers for their views.

Strange as it may seem to us today, none of the women dared to preside over the meeting. James Mott, Lucretia's husband, called the first meeting to order. But it was Elizabeth Cady Stanton who immediately took the floor to lead the discussion. She had prepared 11 resolutions for consideration by the assembly.

Even before the resolutions were presented, there was a heated debate on whether or not to allow men to sign them. The group finally agreed to accept the signatures of the men present but left open the option to reconsider the decision before the convention concluded. (The decision was allowed to stand.)

Elizabeth based her resolutions on a philosophy of natural rights. The first three set the tone of the convention:

1) Resolved: That such laws as conflict, in any way, with the true and substantial happiness of women are contrary to the great precept of nature and of no validity.

2) Resolved: That all laws which prevent woman from occupying such a station in society as her conscience shall dictate, or which place her in a position inferior to that of man, are contrary to the great precept of nature, and therefore of no force or authority.

3) Resolved: That woman is man's equal—was intended to be so by the Creator, and the highest good of the race demands that she should be recognized as such.

More than 100 women and men spent over 18 hours in discussion of the resolutions. The ninth resolution, dealing with the duty of women to secure for themselves the right to vote, caused the most controversy. But even this resolution was passed by a narrow margin before the convention closed.

Few local newspapers reported the convention favorably, but Elizabeth, strengthened by the support she received from Lucretia and her few friends, was undeterred. Just two weeks later she set out for Rochester to attend a similar convention called by Amy Post, a Quaker. At this convention the women broke with tradition and elected Abigail Bush to preside.

Elizabeth probably did not think of herself as carrying out a ministry of community formation, but she certainly became aware of the power of the community that she and her small circle of friends had formed. As they achieved greater freedom for themselves, they struggled valiantly to free all women from many kinds of oppression.

Questions for Reflection

1) What do you think motivated the women gathered for tea to plan a convention?

2) Did this group of women form a community? Is there any indication that the members of the convention felt drawn together as a community? What criteria of a true community did this group meet?

3) What does the fact that James Mott was chosen to preside at the convention tell you about the situation of women at that time? What kind of person do you think he was?

4) What do you think about Elizabeth's resolutions?

Summing Up

The criteria for genuine Christian community present a challenge to modern American Christians living in an individualistic society. At the same time, the very atmosphere of individualism in which we live makes community all the more necessary to counteract our self-centeredness.

The importance of feminine qualities for both community formation and the continued life of the community make this an ideal ministry for women. Although they have a desire for relationships and a gift for nurturing them, women need to realize that genuine Christian community also needs masculine qualities. Loyalty, assertiveness, organizational skills and an overall vision are all needed if the community is to grow and flourish.

Another area of ministry where feminine traits can make a valuable contribution to the Church is the ministry of the Word of God, the focus of the next chapter.

CHAPTER EIGHT

The Feminine and the Ministry of God's Word

*T*he concern in this chapter is the second of Bernard Cooke's categories of ministry—the ministry of God's Word. The ministry of teaching and preaching the Word is carried out in many ways by both men and women. As you read, recall the women who have enriched your life with the Word.

Case: Janet

After many years of serious study, Janet finally received her doctorate in biblical studies. Learning Hebrew and Greek was especially difficult, but she knew she needed these languages for a deeper understanding of Scripture. Now Janet is teaching three courses in Scripture at the seminary. She is respected by her students not only for her knowledge of the Old Testament—her field of specialization—but also for her excellence as a teacher.

Janet has a problem: She cannot bear to sit through the Sunday homily in her parish. The priest touches upon the readings but emphasizes obvious lessons people have heard for years. For Janet, he says nothing alive and fresh. Janet has tried other parishes without much success, but it is apparent to her that many parish priests have not kept up with developments in Scripture studies.

Janet loves the richness of Scripture and longs for the opportunity to share those riches with other parishioners. She has asked several times to give the homily but is always told that women are not allowed to preach. This makes her feel both sad and angry.

Questions for Reflection

1) Do you know any women like Janet who are well qualified to give homilies? How do you suppose they feel about not being able to preach God's Word? Do you think women are justified in feeling oppressed in this situation? Why or why not?

2) How would you feel if a woman gave the homily in your parish next Sunday?

3) In your mind, is there any difference between a sermon and a homily? If so, what are these differences?

4) When you come to Church on Sunday, what expectations do you bring to the homily? Have these expectations been met in the homilies you have heard recently? If not, what was lacking?

5) What feminine qualities do you think would contribute to the effectiveness of a homily?

Gospel Event

Jesus, tired from his journey, sat down there at the well. It was about noon.

A woman of Samaria came to draw water. Jesus said to her, "Give me a drink." ...The Samaritan woman said to him, "How can you, a Jew, ask me, a Samaritan woman, for a drink?" (For Jews use nothing in common with Samaritans.) Jesus answered and said to her, "If you knew the gift of God and who is saying to you, 'Give me a drink,' you would have asked him and he would have given you living water." [The woman] said to him, "Sir, you do not even have a bucket and the cistern is deep; where then can you get this living water? Are you greater than our father Jacob, who gave us this cistern and drank from it himself with his children and his flocks?" Jesus answered and said to her, "Everyone who drinks this water will be thirsty again; but whoever drinks the water I shall give him will never thirst; the water I shall give will become in him a spring of water welling up to eternal life." The woman said to him, "Sir, give me this water, so that I may not be thirsty or have to keep coming here to draw water."

Jesus said to her, "Go call your husband and come back." The woman answered and said to him, "I do not have a husband." Jesus answered her, "You are right in saying,'I do not have a husband.' For you have had five husbands, and the one you have now is not your husband. What you have said is true." The woman said to him, "Sir, I can see that you are a prophet. Our ancestors worshiped on this mountain, but you people say that the place to worship is in Jerusalem." Jesus said to her, "Believe me, woman, the hour is coming when you will worship the Father neither on this mountain nor in Jerusalem." ...The woman said to him, "I know that the Messiah is coming,...when he comes, he will tell us everything." Jesus said to her, "I am he, the one who is speaking with you."

At that moment his disciples returned, and were amazed that he was talking with a woman....The woman left her water jar and went into the town and said to the people, "Come see a man who told me everything I have done. Could he possibly be the Messiah?" They went out of the town and came to him....

Many of the Samaritans of that town began to believe in him because of the word of the woman who testified, "He told me everything I have done." When the Samaritans came to him, they invited him to stay with them; and he stayed there two days. Many more began to believe in him because of his word,...(John 4:6b-21,25-27a, 28-30, 39-41).

Questions for Reflection

1) Trace the steps of the Samaritan woman's growth in faith.

2) What is unusual about Jesus' statement to her: "I who speak

to you am he"?

3) How did Jesus feel about this woman telling the townspeople about him? What evidence do you have for your answer?

4) How did the people respond to the testimony of the woman?

A Closer Look at the Ministry of God's Word

No wonder the disciples were surprised to find Jesus talking to a woman: Jewish men were forbidden to speak to women— even to their own wives—in public. And this woman was a Samaritan. The Samaritans were originally Jews; they had intermarried with pagans at the time of the Babylonian captivity. They were considered unclean by the Jews and therefore all their utensils were also thought to be unclean. Moreover, this woman had a bad reputation in the village. So she came to draw water in the heat of the day when she would not meet the other women.

In spite of these circumstances Jesus takes the initiative in asking for a drink. Then, step by step, he leads this woman to faith. Jesus entrusts her with the wonderful news that she is speaking to the Messiah. Forgetting herself and risking ridicule and rejection, she hurries back to the village to spread the Good News. Through her ministry of God's Word many villagers come to believe in Jesus.

Notice that her ministry of the Word had nothing to do with Scripture. We are inclined to equate God's Word with Scripture. Many good Christians take this approach, seeing the Bible as God's only revealed Word.

But Scripture also contains an element of human experience. It only came to be written because of God's revelation *to human consciousness*. The Hebrew Scriptures are an account of God's progressive self-revelation *and* human response: attempts to be faithful to God, failures to live up to the covenant, experiencing recurrent calls to conversion. So the Hebrew Scriptures are the history of a special people and God's self-revelation in that history.

At a precise moment in history, at the consent of a young

girl, God's self-revelation burst forth as though God could no longer move in small, progressive steps. *The* Word of God is first and foremost the incarnate Second Person of the Trinity—Jesus. Jesus himself is God's Word spoken to us. The life, death and resurrection of Jesus is the message of God's love for us and a pledge of our own resurrection.

The Gospels record this Word. But the Gospels are not Jesus' autobiography. Rather, they give four accounts of his mission from the perspective of his first followers—not merely the facts about Jesus but also how his intimate disciples experienced him.

The Acts of the Apostles and the letters of Paul present the early Church as a community interpreting the Word. This interpretation was not a philosophical reasoning process; it came from their own experience of Jesus and all he meant to them. God reveals himself in our history, too. Our experience needs to be continually interpreted in the light of Scripture, especially the Gospels.

Very early the ministry of God's Word took on two forms in the Church: witness and evangelization. Those who witnessed had walked with Jesus and listened to his message; they knew of his death and resurrection. These people met together to share the Eucharist and to share with one another all that Jesus meant to them. They encouraged and supported one another in their efforts to live the "new way." Their ministry of the Word was not limited to one person or even one group of individuals. Anyone in the Christian community could witness to the Christ-life within.

Beyond these small Christian communities lay a world which had never heard of Jesus. In that world the ministry of the Word was primarily evangelization or teaching. Thus we find Paul traveling from place to place telling the Good News and forming new Christian communities.

Over the centuries teaching has come to dominate the ministry of the Word, not only in missionary regions but even among those who profess the faith. As we pointed out in Chapter Five, all ministries gradually became clericalized (limited to the clergy), including the ministry of the Word. The simple story of the life, death and resurrection of Jesus became so entangled with theological and philosophical systems that the ordinary believer was judged incapable of finding the way safely through the maze. Theologians surfaced as professors of faith and doctrine in seminaries and universities; bishops maintained the authority to judge whether or not theologians' teachings support the Christian faith.

Although the ministry of the Word became largely a masculine ministry, women brought feminine qualities to it. Even though the scope of their ministry was limited, women could minister as Jesus did for the first 30 years of his life: by example. In their homes and in small groups women quietly witnessed to their Christian faith. Because theirs was such an unobtrusive ministry, we may fail to appreciate its power.

Another area of ministry we think traditionally open to women is education. But when congregations of women who focused specifically on education arose in the 18th and 19th centuries, they were a new phenomenon in the Church. These women felt called to dedicate their lives to God not in the cloister but in the classroom, strengthening and revitalizing the faith in Europe.

In France after the turmoil of the Napoleonic Wars, for example, Catholic knowledge and practice were at a low ebb. Julie Billiart began instructing her fellow field-workers during their lunch break. Later, when the Fathers of the Faith (formerly Jesuits; the order was dissolved from 1773-1814) began giving missions to revitalize the faith, Julie was asked to instruct the women. Gradually other young women joined her and she founded the Sisters of Notre Dame de Namur for the education of poor children.

The Catholic school system, the pride of the Church in the United States, flourished largely through the dedicated efforts of such women. The women of many religious congregations who taught in parish schools are largely responsible for keeping alive the faith of immigrants who came to America seeking religious freedom. In parochial and private schools these women are entrusted with the delicate task of developing the faith of the next generation of Catholics. They are ministers of God's Word in the name of education.

These women were always under the authority of the

bishops. As the Catholic school system grew, the bishop's authority was delegated to a priest appointed as superintendent of schools. Not until 1967, when Caroleen Hengen was named superintendent of schools in the Diocese of Dallas, Texas, was a woman even allowed to fill this position.

Some women today are qualified theologians. In universities women are found teaching theology, religious studies, comparative religion—all areas where they bring God's Word to others. They teach in seminaries, too, bringing a feminine influence that will enrich the future ministry of young men preparing for ordination.

The written word has always been an important way of spreading the Good News. The sermons of famous preachers have often been transcribed and circulated to a larger audience. Pious tracts or shorter inspirational pieces exhort and encourage the faithful to a good moral life. Now more and more women who feel called to a ministry of the Word are sharing their feminine perspective of the Christian life through their writings.

Other women are finding new and creative ways to witness to the Word. Often these ministries are rather informal, unstructured and autonomous. Women from all walks of life—homemakers, women religious, career women—come together in Bible study groups, prayer groups, faith-sharing groups, ongoing retreat groups. Frequently their leader is chosen from among the members for her skill in forming and holding together this budding community. Other members may be chosen for special tasks—leading singing or offering opening prayer. In faith-sharing groups especially, each one who speaks of God's action in her life is ministering to the others. In such groups strong bonds of trust and love develop as the members support one another in their response to Christ. The similarities between these groups and the early Christian communities need to be articulated and expanded for the enriched life of the Church.

Another rapidly growing form of the ministry of God's Word is spiritual direction. A dozen years ago this type of ministry was almost totally a masculine ministry. Today more and more women are ministering to Christians eager to grow in their relationship with God. There has been a change, too, in the way men see themselves as spiritual directors. The emphasis is now on listening, being sensitive to God's action in oneself and in the other and gently supporting signs of growth. These concerns of a good director, male or female, all depend on feminine qualities. Any move to dominate, manipulate or make demands can inhibit and even break the director's relationship with the seeker.

Evangelization is taking on a new look, too. Formerly missionaries traveled to distant lands to bring the Good News to those who had never heard of Jesus. Often they imposed their own culture as they preached Christianity. Today those who strive to evangelize others do so with reverence and respect for the customs and habits of the people they serve. The frontier has moved today. It is close at hand in the streets of our large cities, in those who worship the false gods of drugs, excessive wealth, over-ambition for status and power. Through the advances of psychology missionaries to these people know that there is a necessary step to proclaiming the Good News: People must be prepared to think in new ways, to open their minds and hearts to new possibilities before they are ready to hear the message of Jesus.

Questions for Reflection

1) What specific ministries do you consider ministry of God's Word?

2) What specific skills do you think are required for a minister of the Word? Which are masculine and which feminine?

3) Do you agree that the frontier for missionary activity has moved? Where do you encounter this new frontier?

4) Do you think that some people must learn to think in new ways before they can hear the Good News? If so, what are some of the ways you could participate in this "pre-evangelization"?

5) In what ways are you or could you be a minister of the Word?

Illustration: Thomas Merton

Thomas Merton, a Trappist monk who communicated with his fellow monks by an elaborate and complicated sign language, seems an unlikely example of one whose ministry was spreading God's Word. Merton probably wasn't thinking of ministry when he wrote poetry, novels and journals before entering a Kentucky monastery as the United States moved into World War II.

In the first years of his life at Gethsemani, Merton's time was so filled with worship and physical labor that he had no time to think of the world he had left behind. There was certainly no time for writing. Toward the end of his novitiate, Merton's health showed the effects of the rigorous life he was living. His superiors relieved him of much hard manual labor and gave him some French translation to do. Gradually he began writing again.

His autobiography, *The Seven Storey Mountain,* became a best-seller, opening the way to many other books on prayer and the Trappist life. Merton had only a two-hour period each day for writing; it is amazing how much he accomplished in such a limited time. At this time his writing was individualistic; his spirituality sought God by rejecting the world.

Through a long struggle in the late 1950s and early 1960s, Merton changed his stance toward the world. He realized the powerful influence of his words and began to feel he had deluded himself and others. In 1966, he wrote in a *Commonweal* article, "Due to a book I wrote 30 years ago, I have myself become a sort of stereotype of the world-denying contemplative—the man who spurned New York, spat on Chicago, and tromped on Louisville, heading for the woods with Thoreau in one pocket, St. John of the Cross in another, and holding the Bible open at the Apocalypse."

Now the world knew a new Merton as he wrote prolifically on peace and the dangers of a nuclear war. He wrote not just articles and books but also corresponded with statesmen, politicians, journalists, authors and many friends, urging them all to recognize the potential of nuclear weapons to destroy all civilization. He did not hesitate to say that the evil of a nuclear war would be second only to the evil of the crucifixion.

Questions for Reflection

1) Do you believe that Thomas Merton was a minister of the Word when he wrote about seeking God by turning away from the world? Why or why not?

2) Was Merton ministering to the Word through his writings on the dangers of a nuclear war? Why or why not?

3) What feminine qualities are necessary for a minister of the Word? What masculine qualities? Does one or the other predominate?

Summing Up

We have seen how the ministry of the Word can be exercised in a variety of ways—through teaching, witnessing to the Christ-life within, example, spiritual direction, writing. Developments in technology are opening new and exciting possibilities for bringing the Good News to the world. The Church needs both women and men with a variety of talents and skills to use their creativity in this exciting ministry.

In the next chapter we will look at the ministry of service, which also is rich in possibilities for spreading the Reign of God.

CHAPTER NINE

The Feminine and the Ministry of Service

*F*rom the time of Christ to the present day Christians who are true to their call are marked by their love and care for others. As you consider the call to service, consider how masculine and feminine qualities together could complete this third of Cooke's areas of ministry instead of compete with each other.

Case: Sylvia

Sylvia is a newly elected member of St. Monica's parish council. She lives in an affluent neighborhood in a large city. The parish is made up of professional people who contribute generously to their church, enabling the parish to carry on many valuable activities. Last year the parish council decided to assist an inner-city parish in financial and professional matters.

When Sylvia attended her first parish council meeting, the pastor presented the budget for the coming year. Father Romer pointed out that 75 percent of parish income was needed to run the parochial school. He also reported that diocesan authorities were considering establishing a centralized elementary school to serve several parishes. Father Romer asked council members to consider whether St. Monica's should support this plan for restructuring the school district.

Questions for Reflection

1) Do you believe that 75 percent of a parish income is a just proportion to allocate to a school? Why or why not?

2) What benefits might diocesan centralization of parochial schools have for St. Monica's? What sacrifices would have to be made?

3) In what ways could such a decision enable parishioners better to serve the associated inner-city parish?

4) What services do you find lacking in your parish? Which of these services would be rendered best by women? Which by men? Which by a team? Explain your answers.

Gospel Event

So when he had washed their feet [and] put his garments back on and reclined at table again, he said to them, "Do you realize what I have done for you? You call me 'teacher' and 'master,' and rightly so, for indeed I am. If I, therefore, the master and teacher, have washed your feet, you ought to wash one another's feet. I have given you a model to follow so that as I have done for you, you should also do. Amen, amen, I say to you, no slave is greater than his master nor any messenger greater than the one who sent him. If you understand this, blessed are you if you do it (John 13:12-17).

Questions for Reflection

1) How is it possible for Christians today to "wash one another's feet"?

2) Recall that Peter first refused to let Jesus wash his feet. Why do you suppose Peter acted this way? Do you identify with Peter's initial response?

3) Suppose Jesus asks you today, as he once asked Peter,

"Who do you say that I am?" How would you answer him? How does your answer relate to the Gospel passage above? In what way does your answer correspond with your current image of God?

A Closer Look at the Ministry of Service

Since the time of Jesus Christians worthy of the name have cared for others. The death and resurrection of Jesus has continually been presented as the highest expression of love. Christians remember what he said: "This is how all will know that you are my disciples, if you have love for one another." Following Jesus' example, the first Christians expressed their love through service in accordance with the needs of the place and time. Care for the poor, the oppressed, the orphan, the widow became a way of life for those who professed Christianity.

Those in authority within the Christian community not only exhorted their followers to assume responsibility for others' welfare but also themselves strove to be role models. The Epistles emphasize that building unity through the exercise of love is the very heart of the Christian ethic.

Maintaining harmony in relationships required efforts to reconcile differences and the exercise of forgiveness. Extending hospitality to newcomers and strangers and opening one's door to the homeless were characteristic of the authentic followers of Jesus. Caring for and healing the sick—through both medical means and the prayerful laying on of hands—also identified members of the Christian community. Initial and continuing instruction in the faith always accompanied the ministry of service.

Then as now, a ministry of service needed both feminine and masculine characteristics. Service called for compassion, nurturing, intuitive understanding—characteristically feminine responses to needs. So, too, organizational, management and administrative skills—traditionally regarded as masculine traits—were fundamental to harmonious living.

Expressions of love through service came to be called the spiritual and corporal works of mercy. Both women and men engaged in these works, sometimes individually but often in cooperation. As time went on and the number of Christians increased, schools attached to the cathedral and staffed by clerics took responsibility for educating the young. Like-minded individuals began to form religious communities— men and women publicly vowed to poverty, chastity and obedience. They established monastic schools, hospitals, hostels and shelters for travelers.

Today many of the original ministries of the Church have become secularized. Over the centuries, as humanitarian values began to penetrate modern society, many teaching and healing services that began under Church auspices were taken over by secular institutions. We now take it for granted that hospitals and medical centers, schools and social agencies are funded and operated by agencies other than the Church.

Unfortunately, these undertakings, which started as genuine efforts to render service to human beings, sometimes become corrupted by the desire for profit and power. Masculine traits unbalanced by the feminine dimension can make productivity, efficiency and progress more important than human well-being and benefit. Then the task becomes more important than the people performing it or those receiving the service.

The Second Vatican Council cleared the way for an expansion of the Church's services and ministries. It shifted the focus of faith from vertical to horizontal, measuring the relationship with God largely by the character of people's relationship with one another. It put more stress on the responsibility of all God's people, not just clerics and religious, and made human dignity without regard to race, sex, class or culture the foundation of Christian behavior.

In the document *The Church in the Modern World*, the Council also changed the way the Church sees itself in relationship to the world. The Church's separation from the world gives way to its mission *in* the world to bring all to Christ. Rather than encouraging Christians to withdraw into isolation and individualism, the Council urges them to be active in the world, alleviating the sufferings and sorrows of others.

The document on the laity exhorted married and single

persons to recognize their baptismal call to holiness. The document on religious life called on religious congregations to evaluate their lives in the light of gospel values, the charisms of their founders and the signs of the times—in other words, to evaluate the service rendered to those in need in their everyday lives.

The document on the liturgy stressed the horizontal dimension of Catholic worship as well as the vertical, mandating more general participation and communal response. The final blessing at the end of Mass, "go in peace," implies a sending forth to bring the Good News to all people by service to those in need.

Now concerned laypersons and members of religious congregations reach out to attend to new needs our complex society has created and needs neglected by secular institutions. Instead of only operating schools, hospitals and orphanages, believing men and women hear desperate calls from other directions, too. Unemployment, abuse of women and children, teenage pregnancy, homelessness, for example, also call for compassionate response from Jesus' loyal followers.

The needs of the elderly also have become more and more pressing, since our society has made great strides in lengthening lifespan. Many elderly people feel useless, bored and cut off from the mainstream of life. They do not want to spend their time idly just to fill long days. They have led productive lives and want to continue to use their wisdom, experience and talents for others. Creativity in helping people deal with aging has become a challenging new ministry.

Another challenge is the renewal of parishes across the country to provide opportunities for parishioners to deepen their understanding of their responsibility for others. Many people are learning to use their diverse gifts to bring to reality the dream Jesus expressed in his prayer: "so that they may all be one, as you, Father, are in me, and I in you..." (John 17:21). Those who render service in today's Church are signs of hope and evidence that true Christianity is alive and well.

Questions for Reflection

1) How would you respond if someone complained that Catholicism is dying because Vatican II brought about so many changes in the Church?

2) Does your parish support a school? What other kinds of ministry does it offer? What services do you think it should add or drop, and why?

3) In what concrete ways do you practice the corporal and spiritual works of mercy? (Tradition lists seven of each: corporal works of mercy—to feed the hungry, give drink to the thirsty, clothe the naked, shelter the homeless, visit the sick, free prisoners and bury the dead; spiritual works of mercy—to instruct the ignorant, counsel the doubtful, admonish sinners, bear wrongs patiently, forgive offenses, comfort the afflicted and pray for the living and the dead.)

4) How would you describe a "good Catholic?"

Illustration: Senior Gleaners

In Sacramento, California, 2,185 retired people volunteer their services to Senior Gleaners, Inc., an organization dedicated to feeding the needy. Since its beginning in 1976 as a newspaper advertisement placed by a small group of senior citizens, this corporation has inspired similar organizations across the country.

Senior Gleaners salvages millions of tons of food which would otherwise rot and distributes it to the needy. Harvesting methods always leave some fruits and vegetables behind. Farmers call Senior Gleaners when their crops are harvested. Early the next morning volunteers move through the fields gathering all the remaining produce. Only then do the farmers plow and plant for a new crop.

Over age 50 but able-bodied, these men and women also staff warehouses where the food is stored before being delivered to soup kitchens, food pantries and other food centers; keep scrupulous records; and screen organizations for genuine need. Senior Gleaners also take care of former members who are not able to continue to serve.

The gleaners have an irreproachable reputation among the farmers, for they pick only what has been offered. Some farmers plant an extra few rows just to give something more to these gleaners.

Members of Senior Gleaners, Inc., avoid boredom and isolation at the same time they help the less fortunate. They never seem to lack creative initiative but continue to proclaim the Good News through their united efforts.

Questions for Reflection

1) Why do you suppose Senior Gleaners, Inc., caught on so quickly and spread so rapidly through this country?

2) What do you suppose convinced farmers to open their fields to Senior Gleaners, Inc., after gathering their own harvest?

3) In what ways do members of Senior Gleaners, Inc., perform spiritual and corporal works of mercy? In what ways do they affect structures in our country?

4) To whose fields do you suppose the members have greater difficulty gaining access: those engaged in agribusiness or owners of smaller, family-owned farms? Why?

Summing Up

Differing needs in various cultures call forth from Christians a variety of services. Because of the complexity of modern society and modern technology, Christians today have opportunities for service far beyond the neighborhood and even beyond their own country. As Christians try to respond to the signs of the times, it becomes increasingly important that women and men learn to see both feminine and masculine qualities as gifts to be used.

The next chapter will highlight the limitations of the spiritual and corporal works of mercy, and show how ministries of service must be supplemented with ministries of justice.

CHAPTER TEN

The Feminine and the Ministry of Justice

*T*he corporal and spiritual works of mercy—care for the sick, the dying, prisoners, the ignorant, the poor and the troubled—provide temporary assistance to those in a crisis situation. Such short-term help is always needed, but some human problems can be solved only by changing the social structures which cause human suffering. Besides works of charity, Christians are called to works of justice. As you read this chapter, reflect on the role feminine traits play in Cooke's fourth area of ministry: the ministry of justice.

Case: Tom

Five years after his ordination Father Tom was assigned to St. Mary's, an inner-city parish. One night in early December he responded to a sick call. As he was returning to the rectory, he was shocked by the number of people sleeping in doorways and on sidewalk grates—anywhere they might find a little warmth.

When he reached the rectory, Father Tom sat in his car for a few moments to think. Then he restarted the engine and drove slowly through the neighborhood, inviting anyone he saw sleeping outside—including several women with young children—to come to the church. He unlocked the church, turned up the heat a little and told the homeless they could sleep in the pews.

The next morning Father Tom awoke early to consult the pastor about using the church as a shelter for the homeless. Together the priests decided what they must do and then they went to the church to assemble the 50 homeless people. The pastor said, "We wish we could provide permanent shelter for you, but this is a very poor parish. We invite all of you to go with us this morning to the mayor's office. You have a right to shelter and food, and we want the mayor to see what is happening to many people in this city. Changes have to be made."

Questions for Reflection

1) How do you feel about Father Tom's response to the need of the homeless? How would you react if he opened *your* parish church to them?

2) Was Father Tom's response an act of charity or a work of justice? What criteria did you use to decide?

3) In our complicated society, are works of charity adequate to solve social problems? Why or why not?

4) What kind of relationship exists between Father Tom and his pastor? How important are good staff relationships among those working for the poor?

Gospel Event

[Jesus said,] "Woe to you, scribes and Pharisees, you hypocrites. You pay tithes of mint and dill and cummin, and have neglected the weightier things of the law: judgment and mercy and fidelity. [But] these you should have done, without neglecting the others" (Matthew 23:23).

Questions for Reflection

1) What does this passage say about Jesus' attitude toward justice?

2) What relationship do you see between justice, mercy and good faith?

3) How important should justice be in living the Christian life?

4) How do you think the scribes and Pharisees felt when they heard this message? How have you felt when exhorted to works of justice?

A Closer Look at the Ministry of Justice

In 1971 the World Synod of Bishops issued a document called *Justice in the World*. Its opening words state the bishops' intent: "Gathered from the whole world, in communion with all who believe in Christ and with the entire human family, and opening our hearts to the Spirit who is making the whole of creation new, we have questioned ourselves about the mission of the People of God to further justice in the world."

Two significant phrases occur in this opening statement. First, the bishops express their unity with not only other Catholics or even with all Christians but with the entire human family. This was not entirely a new development; just nine days after Vatican II opened, the Council Fathers released a *Message to Humanity* which was, for the first time in the history of ecumenical councils, addressed "to all men and nations." Just a year later Pope John XXIII also addressed his thoughts on peace (*Pacem in Terris*) to the whole world.

These documents recover an ancient biblical emphasis on the relationship of God's people to the world. The Church and the world no longer are seen as separate entities in opposition to one another. Rather, the Church is immersed in the world to bring about the Reign of God for all. By taking this attitude toward the whole human family, the bishops, in a sense, also accepted some responsibility for the welfare of that family.

The second phrase of note is the Spirit "is making the whole of creation new." It appears that one characteristic of this newness is a greater awareness of our unity with all God's children. More than that, advancements in science have made us aware of our bondedness to all of creation—animate and inanimate. The ever-present threats of nuclear disaster, the balance of the world's economy, the greenhouse effect—all these and more make us realize that our lives depend on one another. It is not so much that creation is new as that our vision of creation has changed. The Spirit is working through people in widely scattered areas to use this awareness to build the Kingdom.

In 1971 the bishops were concerned not only about their own mission but also about the mission of the whole People of God. Recalling the discussion of mission and ministry in Chapter Six, it is amazing that the bishops should refer to furthering justice as the *mission* of the People of God. It reflects a deep insight into the relationship between faith and justice that is so clearly enunciated later in the document:

> The mission of preaching the Gospel dictates at the present time that we should dedicate ourselves to the liberation of man even in his present existence in the world. For unless the Christian message of love and justice shows in effectiveness through action in the cause of justice in the world, it will only with difficulty gain credibility with the men of our times. (*Justice in the World*, #35)

Most Catholics are convinced that faith demands charity. But facing this seemingly new demand of faith—action on behalf of justice—makes them decidedly uneasy.

What is involved in works of justice that make them so different from works of charity? Why is justice crucial today?

The answers can be seen in an inner-city center founded 50 years ago to help the poor. For half a century women religious and dedicated lay volunteers have distributed food to the hungry every day at noon—a tremendous work of charity!

But some people coming for their lunch today have been there each day for years. They are no better off now than on the first day they came for help. Their food stamps still run out before the end of the month. They still have no skills to get jobs that pay a living wage and no transportation to where the jobs are. Many people are in poor health; getting off welfare would mean a loss of medical benefits for them.

Working for justice means changing the structures that keep people in poverty—finding ways to provide education, medical care and access to jobs. Meanwhile, charity means working to provide today what justice can't bring about until tomorrow. Changing unjust systems takes time, but people are hungry and need shelter, jobs and medical care *now*. Charity and works of justice are both needed.

Even beginning to think about changing social structures may bring an overpowering sense of frustration and helplessness. An individual cannot change the welfare system or bring peace on earth or prevent contamination of the water supply.

As a matter of fact, an individual ministry of justice seems impossible to sustain. Many who were inspired by the bishops' call to action for justice in the early 1970s responded with enthusiasm, only to experience failure and frustration because they tried to work alone. As more and more people became aware of the need to work for justice, those with similar visions and interests began coming together for support and encouragement. In a very real sense a call to a special ministry of justice implies also a call to a ministry of community formation. If this is the case, then all the qualities needed for the ministry of community formation (see Chapter Seven) are also needed for a justice worker.

Beyond that it may seem at first glance that a ministry of justice requires predominantly masculine qualities: leadership, aggressiveness, logic and political sense. But these qualities need to be balanced by feminine traits: compassion, patience, endurance and commitment to nonviolence. A community of women and men respectful of contributions each can offer is a powerful force to promote justice.

A powerful force is necessary, for resistance can be strong. Every system which oppresses people or threatens the well-being of the planet also benefits some group or individual. The unrewarded labor of peasants enriches a landowner; discrimination against people of a different color enhances the status of their oppressors; the plastics which threaten to bury our planet in waste make life easier for all of us. And the better a system pays off, the greater the threat when someone suggests it be changed.

More than any other ministry, therefore, a commitment to work seriously for justice can be dangerous. Advocates of justice and peace have been harrassed, threatened, spied upon, thrown in prison and even assassinated. Like the prophets of old, courageous women and men today hear and answer God's call and challenge the powerful to be just.

Questions for Reflection

1) Why do you think the bishops speak of being "in communion...with the entire human family"? Are you personally aware of unity with the whole human family? Why or why not?

2) What is the relationship between faith and justice?

3) Give examples from your experience that clarify the differences and similarities between works of charity and works of justice.

4) Is a ministry of justice dangerous? Give examples to support your answer.

5) What feminine and masculine qualities are needed for effective ministry in the examples you just gave?

Illustration: Jean Donovan

Jean Donovan's early life gave little indication of her courageous ministry and martyrdom. Her childhood and adolescent years were spent with her brother in a happy, well-to-do family. She was a good student who loved horseback riding, a hobby her parents could well afford.

As an exchange student in Ireland, Jean met Father Michael Crowley, who recognized in the fun-loving young woman a deep religious sense. He challenged her by his own interest in justice issues.

On her return to the United States, Jean pursued her

business studies and obtained a master's degree in economics. Her first position with a Cleveland accounting firm put her on the executive level at age 24. She did not allow her work to absorb all her thought and time but also became involved in diocesan programs. Through this involvement she learned that the diocese was sponsoring a mission team to El Salvador. In spite of her successful business career, Jean applied for a place on the team.

After finishing her mission preparation, Jean was sent to El Salvador in the summer of 1979. She spent her first year there getting to know the people, trying to understand their situation, doing whatever she could to console families whose fathers and sons had disappeared or been killed.

By the following summer a regular part of the mission team's work was recovering and burying the bodies of the death squads' victims. In October, just a few weeks before her death, Jean wrote in her diary: "Often there is a lot of frustration and pain involved as one cannot do enough, or anything, at times. At times one wonders if one should remain in such a crazy incredible mess. I only know that I am trying to follow where the Lord leads, and in spite of fear and uncertainty at times I feel at peace and hopeful."

On December 4 Jean Donovan and her three companions were brutally raped and murdered. In *U.S. Catholic* Father Crowley summed up the meaning of Jean's life:

> Underneath her happy, casual, nonchalant personality was a serious, committed person with a deep religious conviction, which explained her madness. I mean, by any standards of the 20th century, going down to Salvador and risking your life is a form of madness. But she knew what she was doing, and it fitted totally into her life's meaning, which was a commitment, I think, to her Christianity.

Jean and her companions display a courage and dedication to justice that few of us are called to imitate. But they can inspire us to do *something*, however small it seems, to make our world more just.

Questions for Reflection

1) What do you suppose influenced Jean to become a minister for justice? Do you think there also were influences pulling Jean in another direction?

2) What do you think motivated Jean to go to El Salvador?

3) What feminine qualities operated in Jean?

4) Do you think Jean had any strong masculine qualities? Explain your answer.

5) What opportunities to work for justice are available to you?

Summing Up

In this brief presentation of the ministry of justice we have highlighted the distinction between works of charity and action for justice. Although some people are disturbed by the increased emphasis the Church has given to justice in the last 15 years, it is important to recognize that both justice and charity are needed. The possibilities for ministry through justice work are so numerous that it would be difficult to find any positive quality—feminine or masculine—that would not be an asset in this ministry.

CHAPTER ELEVEN

The Feminine and Sacramental Ministry

A discussion of feminine participation in the last of Bernard Cooke's categories, sacramental ministry, can generate more heat than light. We hope that this brief overview instead will open the way for a balanced discussion.

Case: Doris

Doris is a member of a pastoral team at St. Anne's Hospital. A grueling clinical pastoral education course prepared her for this position. She shares duties with four other pastoral ministers on the team: two sisters, another layperson and a priest.

Doris visits the patients on her assigned floor, brings them Communion, comforts relatives and is on call for eight hours each day. Noted for her ability to listen compassionately, Doris is at times available even during her off-duty hours. Both women and men patients open their hearts to her. Often they bare their consciences to her and beg God's forgiveness for past mistakes.

The priest on the team cannot be as available as Doris because he also has parish duties. Often when patients ask for the Sacrament of Reconciliation, Doris is unable to get in touch with the priest. Doris frequently experiences frustration because she cannot offer absolution.

Questions for Reflection

1) Can you sympathize with Doris' frustration? How would you feel and act in her place?

2) If you were a patient who wanted the Sacrament of Reconciliation, how would you feel if the priest were not available? How do you suppose the priest feels?

3) Can you imagine any way in which this situation might be remedied?

4) Find out, if you can, the projected availability of priests in your diocese. (Call your diocesan newspaper or ask a priest-friend.) How do you feel about this situation?

5) Have you ever been deprived of a sacrament because there was no priest available? How did you react to this deprivation?

Gospel Event

[Jesus prayed:] "Consecrate [my disciples] in the truth. Your word is truth. As you sent me into the world, so I sent them into the world. And I consecrate myself for them, so that they also may be consecrated in truth.

"I pray not only for them, but also for those who will believe in me through their word, so that they may all be one, as you, Father, are in me and I in you, that they also may be in us, that the world may believe that you sent me... and that you loved them even as you loved me" (John 17:17-20, 23b).

Questions for Reflection

1) What do Jesus' words tell you about your relationship with him?

2) Do the sacraments, especially Eucharist and Reconciliation, enable you to unite with all the People of God? How do you experience this effect?

106

3) In your everyday life how can you bring about the realization of Jesus' dream of unity?

4) What connection do you see between belief in Jesus and building a community of faith?

Looking Closer at Sacramental Ministry

From the very beginning Christians, bound by a common vision, came together to worship God. The New Testament offers only slight evidence of the rites of community worship. The first Christians apparently took part in Jewish synagogue services and later celebrated the Eucharist in the context of a meal in their homes.

Now, as then, the Paschal Mystery—the life, death and resurrection of Jesus Christ—is central to Christian faith. Like the first Christians we celebrate the sacrament of the Eucharist as a response to Jesus' Last Supper command to "do this in memory of me" (Luke 22:19b). In the Eucharist the Good News is proclaimed to the Christian community and each member is sent out to carry it to all people. Eucharist forms and unites a community of people who recognize the presence of the risen Jesus in every action of their daily lives.

All the other sacraments are related to the Eucharist; each touches some vital aspect of human experience. Birth, achieving maturity, the need for healing and forgiveness, the experience of love—these basic human experiences are transformed, Christianized, by the sacraments. Six of the seven sacraments are thus related directly to human situations which any woman or man may experience. Only Holy Orders stands apart from ordinary experience.

Each sacrament proclaims the Good News that Jesus Christ is the Son of God and calls for a yes in faith—not only from those assembled in the local community but also from the universal Church. The sacraments thus foster the community of faith and worship, linking today's believers to all those who have gone before, establishing and communicating the apostolic tradition.

But when we consider the *administration* of the sacraments, we have to note that Jesus himself did not belong to the priestly class. Jesus' earthly life was devoted to teaching and healing. Not until after his death on the cross does the author of the Letter to the Hebrews refer to the "great high priest" (see Hebrews 4:14—5:10).

Neither were the apostles thought of primarily in terms of sacramental priesthood. They were first evangelists, proclaimers of God's Word, those who had authority to instruct, to make rules, to judge and to appoint leaders of the community.

As the Church grew, special roles were assigned according to the gifts or talents different individuals possessed. By the third and fourth centuries it seemed fitting to celebrate the ordination of those chosen to administer the sacraments, and rites were formulated to accompany the ceremony. These rites were not looked upon by the community as *giving* the qualities needed to carry out the duties prescribed; ordination *acknowledged* the action of the Holy Spirit already at work in the ordained.

During these years the entire assembled community took part in the sacramental action. The main celebrant acted as a member of this community—not as the cause of the sacramental action, but simply as one given a special role to play.

As years passed, structures were introduced to maintain discipline and good order in the Church in an effort to safeguard the original purity of the faith. From the Council of Nicaea early in the fourth century until the ninth century records indicate that agreement on such structures was reached by bishops gathered together in synod. Before the beginning of the 12th century, the privilege of presiding at sacramental celebrations had nothing to do with the marital status of the minister.

The roots of Christian thinking on clerical celibacy are difficult to trace. As scholars examine the writings of the early Fathers, it is evident that the movement toward celibacy, although based in Scripture, was strongly influenced by a distorted view of the value of the human body and by the prevalent attitude of distrust toward women. In previous chapters we have seen how this discrimination against women affected ministry in the Church. By the fourth century some preachers dealt more often with chastity than with charity.

There is also evidence that economic considerations

influenced the move toward a celibate clergy. In the beginning, when only a few persons were designated to perform duties related to the sacraments, the community could afford to support them. As the Christian population increased and these offices were multiplied, it became necessary to limit the financial support of those in sacramental ministry. Wives and children became a liability and ordained ministers were encouraged to remain celibate. Gradually, celibacy was imposed on the clergy; it became a universal requirement for priests in the Western Church under Pope Gregory VII in the 11th century.

The Gospels say little about celibacy but a great deal about justice and charity. At most, the case for obligatory celibacy of priests seems to rest on weak theological grounds. Some people question the wisdom of the law. May the emphasis on priestly celibacy, they ask, indicate a failure to appreciate the basic goodness of human sexuality and the way the dignity of the human body has been raised by the resurrection of Jesus? Does celibacy create an apparent gap of understanding between the clergy and the other members of the community? They also raise questions about the possible relationship between clerical celibacy and clerical superiority. Unfortunately, many see priestly celibacy as a symbol of masculine domination in the Church.

Many who question the value of priestly celibacy do not deny that those who have a call to celibacy are a gift to the Church. They have witnessed the lives of holy and devoted celibate people and have been deeply influenced by their example and dedication. The problem rises from the fact that the possibility of ordination to the priesthood is *limited* to unmarried men.

Most of the time, that is. At the beginning of our tradition, there is scriptural proof that Peter, chosen by Jesus to be the head of the Church, was married: Jesus cured his mother-in-law (see Mark 1:29-31). In our own time, since the Episcopal Congress in 1977, 40 Episcopalian priests, many of them married, have become Catholic and are continuing their priestly ministry with their wives by their side.

Matrimony is no less a sacrament than Holy Orders. Those who give the sacrament to each other seal their mature love for one another and accept in a deep way the great mystery of the Incarnation. The act of sexual intercourse can foster Christian holiness because it can deepen human love in the context of faith. Bringing new life into being as a consequence of this exchange of human love is one of the most beautiful symbols of human cooperation with God's creative energy. Perhaps no other symbol expresses so well the communication of the divine life made possible because of the Paschal mystery.

If we explore the significance of each of the other sacraments in relation to the basic virtue of love we find both feminine and masculine qualities at work in each. Baptism is birth to new life, a process in which both man and woman have essential roles to play. Confirmation emphasizes the strength and assertiveness often attributed to males as well as the more feminine quality of docility to the Spirit's guidance. Reconciliation and the Sacrament of the Sick call forth compassion and intuitive understanding (regarded as womanly characteristics) along with masculine strength and courage.

Eucharist provides the nourishment which brings about wholeness (integration of masculine and feminine elements) in individuals; it destroys all unequal distinctions within the community and unites men and women in worship and in love. Holy Orders gives the grace to love as Jesus loved, a love demanding both feminine and masculine qualities for its fullest expression. Both feminine and masculine qualities become graced through the reception of the Sacraments.

What is not so clear, at times, is the need for all these graced qualities to be exercised in the Church's ministry. Reserving Holy Orders to celibate men restricts the life-giving effects of the other sacraments. The priest shortage is occurring at a time when contemporary theology stresses the fact that Eucharist is both the sign and cause of unity in the Church. Anything which restricts the opportunity to participate in the Eucharist needs to be seriously evaluated.

As theologian George Worgul writes: "the church is most herself and what she should be in the celebration of the Eucharist. Almost all movements of reform and renewal in the Christian structure have been prophetic demands to return the church to a more real, concrete, and commensurate expression of *communitas* (unity) which should sustain all its dimensions, operations, hopes, designs, and activities." The realization of these prophetic words challenges both women and men to use their talents in the fullest possible way so that the Reign of God may flourish.

Questions for Reflection

1) How have you experienced community when you have witnessed Baptism in your parish church?

2) How has your experience of the new Rite of Reconciliation differed from former confessions?

3) Which of the following words best describes how you feel when you receive the Sacrament of Reconciliation: celebration, encounter, forgiveness, healing? Explain your answer.

4) As you participate in Eucharist, how do you experience relationship with God? With the universal Church? With the others present with you?

5) Compare your responses to the above questions with a person of the opposite sex. Discuss the similarities or differences.

Illustration: Rose Fitzgerald Kennedy

Rose Fitzgerald Kennedy is a valiant woman who enjoys life to the fullest even in the midst of incredible tragedy. The Eucharist has sustained in Rose, a daily communicant, a deep, abiding faith in God's goodness. Others less courageous would have faltered.

According to her autobiography, *Times to Remember*, participation in daily Mass, personal prayer and visits to the Blessed Sacrament, gave Rose needed strength and enabled her to be a channel of fortitude to others. The Eucharist has been the source from which she draws her understanding of God's nature and her own identity. There, too, she has learned the implications of her role as wife, mother and grandmother during good and bad times.

One incident illustrates the impact of the Eucharist on the way Rose lived out her faith life. Rose was weary from participation in her son Bobby's campaign for the presidency in 1968. On June 6, when she awakened at six in the morning in time for Mass, Rose turned on the television to learn how the campaign was going. Instead she was startled by the news that Bobby was on his way to the hospital after having been shot. Remembering that awful day, Rose wrote:

> It seemed impossible that the same kind of disaster could befall our family twice in five years. If I had read anything of the sort in fiction I would have put it aside as incredible. I still wanted to go to Mass—though Ann told me the phones had been ringing and photographers would be at the church....
>
> Monsignor Thomas rode back from church with me. I really don't remember what was said or much of what I was thinking except that I was praying, "Lord, have mercy," and thinking, "Oh Bobby, Bobby, Bobby."

Robert Kennedy's tragic death called forth in Rose once again the strength of one who was bonded in faith, hope and love with a crucified God. The press commented again and again on her composure, self-possession and bravery. During the funeral procession, as she rode through the crowds assembled to pay tribute to Bobby, she waved to the people on the route and encouraged those with her to do the same. She wondered if others might consider such an action inappropriate, but she wanted to show appreciation to those who also mourned the death of her son.

Toward the end of her autobiography, Rose sums up the whole thrust of her long life: "If God were to take away all his blessings, health, physical fitness, wealth, intelligence, and leave me with but one gift, I would ask for faith—for faith in Him, in His goodness, mercy, love for me, and belief in everlasting life." Rose Fitzgerald Kennedy's estimate of herself and her values reveals how well she grasped the many gifts given her.

Questions for Reflection

1) How would you have responded to Rose Kennedy's waving to people along the route of her son's funeral procession? Why?

2) What does Rose's urgent desire to attend Mass the day of Bobby's death reveal about her faith life?

3) What would you have done in Rose's place?

4) What does Rose's attitude toward the Eucharist in her life say to you now?

Summing Up

As the number of Christians increased, it became necessary to institute structures and formulate laws in order to maintain discipline and safeguard the deposit of faith. In the current vocations crisis these institutions sometimes restrict access to the sacraments. In spite of papal pronouncements, therefore, questions still are being raised about the relevance and effectiveness of some of these laws and structures.

Questions for Reflection

Chapter One: Defining Femininity

CASE: CARL

1) How would Carl's business associates describe him? How would a neighbor, observing Carl with the children, describe him? Explain any differences.

2) How do you think Carl would feel if his business associates saw him caring for the children?

3) Do you think Carl is typical of young executives? Explain your answer.

4) At work, Carl has a reputation for clear, logical thinking. Are there other ways of thinking? Are these ways appropriate for the business world?

5) Do you usually arrive at decisions logically or by consulting your feelings? Do you always arrive at decisions in the same way? Explain your answer.

GOSPEL EVENT

1) The disciples and Jesus responded to children in very different ways. How do you explain this difference?

2) How do you think children reacted to the disciples? How do you suppose the children's mothers felt toward the disciples?

3) How do you picture children responding to Jesus? Can you sense how the mothers felt toward Jesus?

4) Do you believe that there are feminine traits and masculine traits? If so, try to list 10 of each.

5) What is the source of these traits?

A CLOSER LOOK AT FEMININITY

1) As you reflect on your own personality, list 10 traits that you find in yourself. Label each trait feminine or masculine. How did you decide which traits are feminine and which are masculine?

2) Choose one feminine trait and one masculine trait that you find in yourself. Try to trace the development of these traits in your life, starting with your childhood.

3) Do you think it is important to recognize and accept both aspects of your personality—the feminine and masculine? Why?

ILLUSTRATION: GOLDA MEIR

1) What positive feminine qualities did Golda seem to exhibit? What positive masculine qualities?

2) Would you be comfortable working with someone like Golda? Explain.

3) Have you ever known a woman in whom masculine as well as feminine qualities were highly visible?

Chapter Two: The Feminine Side of God

1) Why do you think some people are upset when Erica uses inclusive language?

2) Do you think it is important to use inclusive language at Eucharist? Why or why not?

3) Explore your image of God with this exercise: List adjectives you use to describe God. Which denote masculine qualities and which describe feminine traits? Which kind dominate your description of God?

GOSPEL EVENT

1) Notice phrases in the Gospel story which describe Jesus' actions: "moved with pity," "do not weep," "touched the coffin," "gave him back to his mother." What adjectives could you use to describe Jesus in this event?

2) Notice the words used by the people in the crowd: "A great prophet..."; "God has visited his people." What virtues are displayed by the people who respond this way?

3) Considering that Jesus is God, are there any hints of the divine feminine in this incident?

A CLOSER LOOK AT THE FEMININE SIDE OF GOD

1) What is your clearest image of God? Is that a masculine or feminine image?

2) Which biblical images of God appeal to you most? Why?

3) What effect do you think stressing masculine images of God has had on Christianity?

4) How can reflecting on the feminine images of God enrich your relationship with God?

ILLUSTRATION: ANN SULLIVAN MACY

1) How does the relationship between Ann and Helen mirror

the feminine qualities of God?

2) In what ways have specific persons in your life brought you to new psychological and spiritual growth?

3) In what relationships have you called forth life in others?

4) How would you characterize the early relationship between Ann and Helen? Did this relationship change? Have you had any similar experiences?

Chapter Three: The Feminine Side of Jesus

CASE: JOHN

1) Is John's way of treating the homeless appropriate? Why or why not?

2) How do you feel about the director's attitude toward the homeless who come to the shelter?

3) Are there unspoken implications in the director's statement? If so, what do these implications tell you about the director?

4) Imagine yourself in John's place. What would you do?

5) Think of five persons you encountered in the past week and reflect on your interaction with each one. Was the person a woman or a man? What qualities did this person call forth from you? Did you feel you were your true self with this person, or did you respond the way you thought the person expected? What was the outcome of this encounter for each of you? How do you explain any differences among the five encounters?

GOSPEL EVENT

1) Is it reasonable that a man would leave 99 sheep untended and unprotected to go in search of one? Why or why not?

2) What kind of man is Jesus portraying in this parable?

3) What does Jesus reveal about himself and his Father in this parable?

1) How do you feel about reflecting on Jesus in terms of modern psychology?

2) Find several passages in the Gospels that show Jesus' masculine traits in contrast to the feminine qualities presented in this chapter. What other miracles do you feel reveal his masculine qualities? How do they differ from the ones cited in this chapter?

3) How do you understand the "Kingdom" or "Reign" of God? Does your description of the Kingdom contain both feminine and masculine aspects?

4) Read slowly Dorothy L. Sayers' comment about Jesus. How do you feel about Jesus as you read this?

ILLUSTRATION: TEILHARD DE CHARDIN

1) What similarities do you find in Teilhard's approach to his mission and Jesus' desert preparation for his?

2) Do you believe that Teilhard followed the example of Jesus in carrying out his mission? If so, in what ways?

3) Do you find any evidence that Teilhard was in touch with his unconscious feminine traits?

4) Are there any similarities in the consequences of Jesus' and Teilhard's loyalty to their respective missions?

5) Do you believe that Teilhard's attitude toward the Church is relevant for Catholics today? Why or why not?

Chapter Four: Feminine Influence in the Early Church

CASE: CHRISTA AND JOHN

1) Do you share in the disappointment experienced by Christa and John? Why or why not?

2) Why do you think that Christa was not welcome to participate fully in the permanent deacon program?

3) Do you believe that the People of God would benefit more if Christa and John could work together than if John ministers alone as a permanent deacon? Why or why not?

4) From your observation, are more men or more women actively involved in ministry in your parish? Can you think of reasons why this is true?

5) Are there any ministries that you think are being neglected in your parish? If so, what can you do to remedy the situation?

GOSPEL EVENT

1) What do you suppose Mary meant to do when she reached the tomb? Was this reasonable?

2) Do you believe that a compassionate response is usually called forth by a reasoning process? Why or why not?

3) How do you feel when your friends call you by name? Is your response similar to Mary's?

4) How do you suppose Mary felt as Jesus said, "Stop holding on to me"?

5) How do you think Mary felt when she heard Jesus say, "Go...and tell them..."? When have you been sent to bring the Good News to others?

6) Bernard of Clairvaux once called Mary Magdalene an "apostle to the apostles." Do you think this is a good title for Mary? Why or why not?

A CLOSER LOOK AT THE EARLY CHURCH

1) The early Church developed a model of ministry in which men and women worked together in service to the Christian community. What evidence of such cooperation do you observe in your own parish? What evidence of competition between the sexes do you see in your parish?

120

2) Envision ways Christianity can further cooperation rather than competition. Who in your parish exemplifies such a vision?

3) What feminine qualities help to bring about cooperation rather than competition?

4) How could the women of your parish help create a more Christian community?

5) If deaconesses were once so prominent in Church ministry, why do you think women are now excluded from the permanent diaconate?

ILLUSTRATION: SIMONE WEIL

1) In what ways was Simone like the early Christians? In what ways was she different?

2) Why do you think Simone felt she had no choice in putting off Baptism?

3) What masculine qualities do you see in Simone? What feminine qualities?

4) How have you carried out your search for truth?

Chapter Five: The Decline of Feminine Influence

CASE: CARLOS

1) In what ways have you heard God's call as you prayed over Scripture passages?

2) These peasants were neither Scripture scholars nor theologians. What does this tell you about the power of the Word of God?

3) In your parish what pastoral activities could be assumed by lay women and men? In what areas would feminine qualities enrich this pastoral care?

1) What feminine qualities did Jesus show in his conversation with the lawyer?

2) Why do you think the priest and the Levite passed by the man?

3) The Jews looked upon the Samaritans with contempt. In his story why do you think Jesus chose a Samaritan to help the injured traveler?

4) Who might 20th-century Americans look upon as Samaritans? Why?

A CLOSER LOOK AT THE DECLINE OF FEMININE INFLUENCE

1) Where does the power of decision rest in your parish?

2) Are both men and women well represented on your parish council? How are the members selected?

3) Is it necessary to have structure in an institution as large as the Roman Catholic Church? How and by whom should decisions be made within such a structure?

4) In your lifetime have you observed a lessening of patriarchy in the Church at any level—parish, diocese, universal Church? Present the evidence.

5) In what ways has the decreasing number of priests affected your life?

ILLUSTRATION: ELIZABETH BAYLEY SETON

1) Has your loyalty to a parish priest or bishop ever been challenged by an apparent injustice? If so, what have you done about it?

2) Do you know people who have spoken in opposition to an unjust act? How have you responded to such people?

3) Do you believe it is possible for a good Christian to have a radically different point of view than a pastor or bishop?

How can such contrary views be expressed in a respectful and open manner?

4) How do you view dissent in the institutional Church?

Chapter Six: Vatican II and Rewaking the Feminine

CASE: BILL AND SUE

1) Would you have reacted to the homily more like Bill or like Sue? Why?

2) What does the image "Holy Mother Church" imply to you?

3) Do you think it is important what image we use for the Church? Explain.

4) List the images of the Church you have heard or encountered in your reading. Next to each image list as many qualities associated with that image as you can. Which image of the Church appeals to you most? Why?

5) Does any one image imply all the qualities you look for in the Church? If not, what qualities are missing from your favorite image?

GOSPEL EVENT

1) As Jesus describes his mission in Isaiah's words, what strikes you about the passage?

2) How do you see the mission of Jesus being continued in the world today?

3) Quoting Isaiah, Jesus summarizes his mission in terms of the poor, captives, the blind and prisoners. If Jesus were describing his mission today, what other groups of people might he mention?

4) Why do you think all the people in the synagogue were so fascinated with Jesus?

1) Do you believe that you are co-responsible for the mission of Christ? If so, what is your responsibility? How do you carry it out?

2) For each of Cooke's five categories, list as many specific ministries as you can. Compare your list with the lists of other group members.

3) Do you feel that you have a ministry in the Church? Why or why not?

4) Do you believe that a baptized Christian can minister to others without being officially appointed to the ministry? Why or why not?

ILLUSTRATION: CATHERINE DE HUECK DOHERTY

1) What kinds of ministry do you find in Catherine's story?

2) What difference do you think Catherine saw between her poverty as a refugee and her poverty in Harlem?

3) If Catherine were beginning her work in Harlem today, what do you think she would call her "chitchat apostolate?"

4) Do you believe Catherine's "chitchat apostolate" was really ministry? Why or why not?

Chapter Seven: The Feminine and the Ministry of Building Community

CASE: CAROL

1) Would you call Carol's working pilgrimage a "ministry"? Why or why not?

2) What qualities must Carol have to make her dream come true? Are these qualities feminine or masculine?

3) Do you consider the group of lawyers which Carol has recruited a community? Why or why not?

4) What is your definition of community? Using your own criteria, list all the communities to which you belong and rank them in the order of their importance to you.

5) What criteria did you use in ranking the communities to which you belong?

6) Were you responsible for forming any of these communities? If so, what was your contribution?

7) Are you a leader in any of these communities? What responsibilities do you have as a leader?

8) Next to each of the communities you have listed, indicate the qualities that are important in a member. Are these qualities masculine, feminine or a combination of both?

GOSPEL EVENT

1) What qualities of community do you find in this incident?

2) Do you find any qualities of a genuine community missing in this event?

3) It is obvious that Jesus is the leader of the apostles' community. How does he show his leadership? How do the apostles respond?

4) What adjectives would you use to describe Jesus' leadership? Do these adjectives describe masculine or feminine traits?

LOOKING CLOSER AT COMMUNITY FORMATION

1) Reflect on each of the communities to which you belong, applying Royce's criteria for genuine community. What conclusions do you draw from your reflection?

2) Do you think Royce's criteria are too idealistic? Why or why not?

3) Make a list of masculine and feminine qualities necessary for a viable community. What does this list tell you about the members?

4) Do you believe it is difficult to form genuine community?

Why or why not? What would you find most difficult and how might you go about resolving this difficulty?

5) Why is community formation an important ministry in the Church? Do you think you have gifts for this kind of ministry?

1) What do you think motivated the women gathered for tea to plan a convention?

2) Did this group of women form a community? Is there any indication that the members of the convention felt drawn together as a community? What criteria of a true community did this group meet?

3) What does the fact that James Mott was chosen to preside at the convention tell you about the situation of women at that time? What kind of person do you think he was?

4) What do you think about Elizabeth's resolutions?

Chapter Eight: The Feminine and the Ministry of God's Word

CASE: JANET

1) Do you know any women like Janet who are well qualified to give homilies? How do you suppose they feel about not being able to preach God's Word? Do you think women are justified in feeling oppressed in this situation? Why or why not?

2) How would you feel if a woman gave the homily in your parish next Sunday?

3) In your mind, is there any difference between a sermon and a homily? If so, what are these differences?

4) When you come to Church on Sunday, what expectations do you bring to the homily? Have these expectations been met in the homilies you have heard recently? If not, what was lacking?

5) What feminine qualities do you think would contribute to the effectiveness of a homily?

1) Trace the steps of the Samaritan woman's growth in faith.

2) What is unusual about Jesus' statement to her: "I who speak to you am he"?

3) How did Jesus feel about this woman telling the townspeople about him? What evidence do you have for your answer?

4) How did the people respond to the testimony of the woman?

A CLOSER LOOK AT THE MINISTRY OF GOD'S WORD

1) What specific ministries do you consider ministry of God's Word?

2) What specific skills do you think are required for a minister of the Word? Which are masculine and which feminine?

3) Do you agree that the frontier for missionary activity has moved? Where do you encounter this new frontier?

4) Do you think that some people must learn to think in new ways before they can hear the Good News? If so, what are some of the ways you could participate in this "pre-evangelization"?

5) In what ways are you or could you be a minister of the Word?

ILLUSTRATION: THOMAS MERTON

1) Do you believe that Thomas Merton was a minister of the Word when he wrote about seeking God by turning away from the world? Why or why not?

2) Was Merton ministering to the Word through his writings on the dangers of a nuclear war? Why or why not?

3) What feminine qualities are necessary for a minister of the

Word? What masculine qualities? Does one or the other predominate?

Chapter Nine: The Feminine and the Ministry of Service

CASE: SYLVIA

1) Do you believe that 75 percent of a parish income is a just proportion to allocate to a school? Why or why not?

2) What benefits might diocesan centralization of parochial schools have for St. Monica's? What sacrifices would have to be made?

3) In what ways could such a decision enable parishioners better to serve the associated inner-city parish?

4) What services do you find lacking in your parish? Which of these services would be rendered best by women? Which by men? Which by a team? Explain your answers.

GOSPEL EVENT

1) How is it possible for Christians today to "wash one another's feet"?

2) Recall that Peter first refused to let Jesus wash his feet. Why do you suppose Peter acted this way? Do you identify with Peter's initial response?

3) Suppose Jesus asks you today, as he once asked Peter, "Who do you say that I am?" How would you answer him? How does your answer relate to the Gospel passage above? In what way does your answer correspond with your current image of God?

A CLOSER LOOK AT THE MINISTRY OF SERVICE

1) How would you respond if someone complained that Catholicism is dying because Vatican II brought about so many changes in the Church?

2) Does your parish support a school? What other kinds of ministry does it offer? What services do you think it should add or drop, and why?

3) In what concrete ways do you practice the corporal and spiritual works of mercy? (Tradition lists seven of each: corporal works of mercy—to feed the hungry, give drink to the thirsty, clothe the naked, shelter the homeless, visit the sick, free prisoners and bury the dead; spiritual works of mercy—to instruct the ignorant, counsel the doubtful, admonish sinners, bear wrongs patiently, forgive offenses, comfort the afflicted, and pray for the living and the dead.)

4) How would you describe a "good Catholic?"

ILLUSTRATION: SENIOR GLEANERS

1) Why do you suppose Senior Gleaners, Inc., caught on so quickly and spread so rapidly through this country?

2) What do you suppose convinced farmers to open their fields to Senior Gleaners, Inc., after gathering their own harvest?

3) In what ways do members of Senior Gleaners, Inc., perform spiritual and corporal works of mercy? In what ways do they affect structures in our country?

4) To whose fields do you suppose the members have greater difficulty gaining access: those engaged in agribusiness or owners of smaller, family-owned farms? Why?

Chapter Ten: The Feminine and the Ministry of Justice

CASE: TOM

1) How do you feel about Father Tom's response to the need of the homeless? How would you react if he opened *your* parish church to them?

2) Was Father Tom's response an act of charity or a work of justice? What criteria did you use to decide?

3) In our complicated society, are works of charity adequate to solve social problems? Why or why not?

4) What kind of relationship exists between Father Tom and his pastor? How important are good staff relationships among those working for the poor?

1) What does this passage say about Jesus' attitude toward justice?

2) What relationship do you see between justice, mercy and good faith?

3) How important should justice be in living the Christian life?

4) How do you think the scribes and Pharisees felt when they heard this message? How have you felt when exhorted to works of justice?

1) Why do you think the bishops speak of being "in communion...with the entire human family"? Are you personally aware of unity with the whole human family? Why or why not?

2) What is the relationship between faith and justice?

3) Give examples from your experience that clarify the differences and similarities between works of charity and works of justice.

4) Is a ministry of justice dangerous? Give examples to support your answer.

5) What feminine and masculine qualities are needed for effective ministry in the examples you just gave?

1) What do you suppose influenced Jean to become a minister for justice? Do you think there also were influences pulling

Jean in another direction?

2) What do you think motivated Jean to go to El Salvador?

3) What feminine qualities operated in Jean?

4) Do you think Jean had any strong masculine qualities? Explain your answer.

5) What opportunities to work for justice are available to you?

Chapter Eleven: The Feminine and Sacramental Ministry

CASE: DORIS

1) Can you sympathize with Doris' frustration? How would you feel and act in her place?

2) If you were a patient who wanted the Sacrament of Reconciliation, how would you feel if the priest were not available? How do you suppose the priest feels?

3) Can you imagine any way in which this situation might be remedied?

4) Find out, if you can, the projected availability of priests in your diocese. (Call your diocesan newspaper or ask a priest-friend.) How do you feel about this situation?

5) Have you ever been deprived of a sacrament because there was no priest available? How did you react to this deprivation?

GOSPEL EVENT

1) What do Jesus' words tell you about your relationship with him?

2) Do the sacraments, especially Eucharist and Reconciliation, enable you to unite with all the People of God? How do you experience this effect?

3) In your everyday life how can you bring about the realization

of Jesus' dream of unity?

4) What connection do you see between belief in Jesus and building a community of faith?

LOOKING CLOSER AT SACRAMENTAL MINISTRY

1) How have you experienced community when you have witnessed Baptism in your parish church?

2) How has your experience of the new Rite of Reconciliation differed from former confessions?

3) Which of the following words best describes how you feel when you receive the Sacrament of Reconciliation: celebration, encounter, forgiveness, healing? Explain your answer.

4) As you participate in Eucharist, how do you experience relationship with God? With the universal Church? With the others present with you?

5) Compare your responses to the above questions with a person of the opposite sex. Discuss the similarities or differences.

ILLUSTRATION: ROSE FITZGERALD KENNEDY

1) How would you have responded to Rose Kennedy's waving to people along the route of her son's funeral procession? Why?

2) What does Rose's urgent desire to attend Mass the day of Bobby's death reveal about her faith life?

3) What would you have done in Rose's place?

4) What does Rose's attitude toward the Eucharist in her life say to you now?

For Further Reading

Bellah, Robert N., et al. *Habits of the Heart*. New York: Harper and Row, 1986.

Brown, Raymond E. *The Church the Apostles Left Behind*. New York: Paulist Press, 1984.

Cooke, Bernard. *Sacraments and Sacramentality*. Mystic, Connecticut: Twenty-Third Publications, 1983.

Fiorenza, Elizabeth Schussler. *In Memory of Her*. New York: Crossroad Publishing Company, 1983.

Mollenkott, Virginia Ramey. *The Divine Feminine*. New York: Crossroad Publishing Company, 1984.

Moloney, Francis J., S.D.B. *Woman, First Among the Faithful*. Notre Dame, Indiana: Ave Maria Press, 1986.

Pearsall, Marilyn. *Readings in Recent Feminist Philosophy*. Belmont, California: Wadsworth Publishing Company, 1986.

Ruether, Rosemary Radford. *Sexism and God-Talk*. Boston: Beacon Press, 1983.

Russell, Letty, M. *Human Liberation in a Feminist Perspective— A Theology*. Philadelphia: Westminster Press, 1974.

Schillebeeckx, Edward. *The Mission of the Church*. New York: Seabury Press, 1973.

Swidler, Leonard. *Biblical Affirmations of Woman*. Philadelphia: Westminster Press, 1979.

Worgul, S. George. *From Magic to Metaphor*. Lanham, Maryland: University Press of America, Inc., 1985.